Judith Blackstone, MA, has been an innovative teacher and writer in the psycho-spiritual field for over two decades. She is the founder of Subtle Self Work, a method of realizing non-dual consciousness and applying it to physical and psychological healing. She is on the faculty of Esalen Institute in Big Sur, California and director of Realization Center in Woodstock, New York. She is author of *The Subtle Self: Personal Growth and Spiritual Practice* and *The Enlightenment Process: How it Deepens Your Experience of Self, Body and Community* and co-author of *Zen for Beginners*. She lives in Woodstock, New York.

For Zoran, with love for your pilgrim soul

Living Intimately

*A Guide to Realizing Spiritual
Unity in Relationships*

JUDITH BLACKSTONE

WATKINS PUBLISHING
LONDON

This edition published in the UK in 2002 by
Watkins Publishing, 20 Bloomsbury Street,
London, WC1B 3QA

Cover design by Echelon Design, Wimborne
Cover photograph © Telegraph Colour Library
Author photograph © Laura Kavanau
Designed and typeset by Echelon Design, Wimborne
Printed and bound in Great Britain by NFF Production

British Library Cataloguing in Publication data available

Library of Congress Cataloging in Publication data
available

ISBN 1 84293 033 8

Contents

Introduction

To love life, and in particular to love other human beings, is one of the central ideals of every spiritual tradition. It is also one of life's greatest challenges. Love requires us to be real. Its source is the essence of our being that is somehow hidden or enfolded within us. Our desire and our efforts to love uncover the mysterious wound of separation from our authentic self. For this reason, our relationships can help us realize the spiritual essence of ourselves.

For many people the word 'spiritual' suggests an intangible, inaccessible and perhaps improbable realm of existence. As spirituality is understood in this book, however, it is our true and basic nature, beneath the fantasies, artifices and constraints that distort our usual experience. It is our most subtle and most clear attunement to ourselves and the world around us.

Although it cannot be detected within the ordinary range of our senses, the subtle essence of our being does become tangible as we attune to it. It becomes an actual experience, a quality of being that is felt in our whole body, and that can then be discerned in all of life. As we realize this essence of ourselves, our senses themselves become more subtle, revealing a radiance, fluidity and spaciousness that suffuses the material world. The most radical transformation that occurs with this subtle attunement is that, instead of experiencing ourselves as separate from our environment, we find that our own being is continuous with everything around us. This book describes how the realization of this unified, spiritual dimension of life transforms all of our relationships.

It focuses especially on relationships with an intimate partner.

The understanding that I present in this book is most closely aligned with the Hindu system of Advaita (nondual) Vedanta and the Tibetan Buddhist teachings of Mahamudra and Dzog-chen. It is also informed, however, by the accumulated knowledge of Western psychology, by old and new methods of body/mind healing and by my own experience of spiritual practice. I am not concerned with arguing for a particular philosophy, for I do not believe we can know for certain which explanation of ultimate reality is most true. I do know that the experience of spiritual oneness is the innate potential of our human organism, and that it involves a transformation of every aspect of ourselves, including our physical body and our psychological maturity.

Spiritual realization is not a matter of constructing something new; it is always a clearing away, or a letting go of the holding patterns and beliefs that obscure our true nature. If oneness is our true nature, it is also the natural potential, the underlying reality, of our relationships with other people. This book looks at how relationships can help both partners in a relationship release their barriers to spiritual oneness. This is presented as a dual process of resolving our resistances to contact with our partner and of attuning directly to the subtle dimension of spiritual unity.

The spiritual essence of life is our most subtle, fundamental dimension of consciousness. The Hindu literature describes fundamental consciousness as all-pervasive. It is experienced as vast space, pervading our own form and everything else that we experience – even physical space itself. It is therefore the basis of unity within our own being, our internal wholeness. And it is the basis of the unity of our own being with everything around us. It is an unbroken dimension, a dimension of wholeness and stillness that, when we attune to it, is co-existent with the movement of life. Spiritual realization is not just a matter of uplifting our mood, or changing our behaviors and beliefs. It means that we enter into, and experience ourselves as, the spiritual dimension of existence.

Although the traditional teachings do not speak of it in this way, fundamental consciousness is the basis of contact – our deepest contact with ourselves, with other people, and with all of nature. The ability to love goes beyond having an emotional response to or understanding of another person. It requires the capacity for contact. Every aspect of ourselves is capable of contact, including our touch, gaze, voice, emotions, and awareness. Human beings crave this contact instinctively, for everything that it reaches becomes awake, alive. When we enter the spiritual path, we are learning to love. We are developing this capacity for contact.

Although our fundamental dimension of consciousness is referred to in spiritual teachings, it is just beginning to gain recognition in the psychological field. Up until recently it was thought, in the more adventurous schools of psychology, physics and medicine, that energy was the basic stratum of life. Energy is easier to perceive and to feel than consciousness. It is a less subtle level of ourselves than consciousness, and requires a less subtle attunement in order to experience it. Therefore, the application of fundamental consciousness to psychological and physical healing represents the cutting edge of the human growth movement.

There is also a growing recognition in contemporary psychology of the mutuality, or interconnectedness, of existence. The psychoanalytic theorist, Robert D. Stolorow, describes human interaction as an 'intersubjective field' of mutual influence. Interestingly, Buddhist philosopher, David Loy[1],

---

1 David Loy, *Nonduality* (Amherst, NY: Humanity Books, 1998)

refers to the unified, spiritual dimension as a 'pre-subjective ground'. In this book, I describe how the intersubjective field can gradually transform into the 'pre-subjective' field of spiritual oneness. I also show how this shift brings compassion and insight to relationships, and helps both partners disentangle themselves from the defenses and projections that obstruct the flow of exchange between them.

Human development can be seen as a gradual realization of the relational field. In this process, we develop inward contact and the capacity for contact with other people at the same time. It begins in infancy, as the rudimentary distinction between self-awareness and awareness of our mother, or primary caretaker, and culminates in the simultaneous self-knowledge and oneness with others that defines spiritual maturity. This book looks at the difficulties that thwart this developmental process and how they can lead to the boundary problems of merging with (loss of self-contact) and distancing from others. It also shows how the realization of fundamental consciousness resolves these difficulties, so that our development towards spiritual oneness can proceed.

One of the main barriers to contact in intimate relationships is the fear that we will become submerged in another person. Attunement to fundamental consciousness can alleviate this fear because it is the basis of contact with ourselves as well as with other people. Fundamental consciousness pervades both our internal being and our environment as a unified whole. When we live in this dimension, we have a felt sense of both our internal experience and our oneness with the life around us at the same time. We can therefore experience oneness with another person while remaining attuned to our own internal being. Spiritual oneness is not a loss of self in the other, not the merging of identities that is so often a problem for people in relationships. It is the unity, and continuity, of two individual people. In the dimension of fundamental consciousness we grow simultaneously towards wholeness within our own body and towards oneness with other people.

We can enter into spiritual oneness through a subtle channel that runs through the vertical core of the body. This channel is the center of the chakra system in Hindu yoga and is called *sushumna*. In Buddhism it is called 'the central channel'. The subtle core of our body is both our deepest connection with ourselves and the basis of our oneness with other people. In the dimension of spiritual oneness, partners can relate with each other 'core-to-core'. This releases a flow of subtle energies between them which provides a non-verbal foundation for communication.

Through the subtle core of our body we can also develop the essential qualities of our being. In this book I define the three primary qualities of our being as awareness, emotion (or love) and physical sensation. These are also the three major pathways of our contact with other people. As we realize the spiritual foundation of life, we experience contact with other people as a continuity of awareness, emotion and physical sensation.

Most people have more access to just some of these essential qualities rather than all of them. For example, they may be able to experience emotional and mental contact with another human being, but physical sensation is more difficult. When two people feel out of contact with each other, or when they reach an impasse in their communication, it is often because they are each open to different aspects of contact. The realization of fundamental consciousness balances and integrates these three essential qualities of being, making contact and communication between partners easier, and more complete. Also, the process of two people opening to each other in the realms of sensation, love and awareness can facilitate, for both of them, the path towards spiritual oneness.

The realization of fundamental consciousness gradually transforms the functioning of our senses. It is as if our senses are washed clean of our habitual ways of focusing on the world, and stripped of the mental elaborations that usually accompany our perceptions. The traditional spiritual literature of the East calls this 'direct' or 'bare' perception. We feel that, for the first time, we are perceiving the world as it really is. Our senses also become more refined and, as I have said, they reveal a more subtle world. Everything that we perceive appears to be made of energy and consciousness.

This bare perception is part of our oneness with other people. Usually we see and touch only from the surface of ourselves to the surface of other people, but in fundamental consciousness we are able to see and to touch beneath the surface to the feelings and qualities within. We are able to hear the qualities of a person's whole being in the sound of their voice, or to feel them in the sensation of their touch. With an intimate partner, bare perception can provide the basis of deep understanding and attunement.

Spiritual oneness also brings a deepened perspective and compassion to one of the main stumbling blocks in relation-ships – coping with each other's childhood wounds and defenses. In the clear, pervasive space of fundamental consciousness, it becomes much easier to recognize and release the defenses, beliefs and behaviors that prevent us from experiencing contact with another person. Wherever, in our own organism, we are not available for contact, we are also unable to experience the stillness, spaciousness and unity of the spiritual dimension. Therefore, there is a direct correlation between psychological maturity (the dissolution of defenses and projections) and spiritual realization.

Attunement to fundamental consciousness also helps release

the psychological holding patterns that diminish sexual pleasure. It can help people tolerate a greater intensity of stimulation, and achieve more genuine, and therefore more pleasurable, sexual contact. Physical sensation is an inseparable part of the essence of our being, and of our spiritual oneness with other life. The limitation which many people experience in their capacity for sexual pleasure is also a barrier to the realization of spiritual oneness.

In some Tantric traditions, partners use the energy of sexual release to 'fuel' the rise of energy through their bodies. These exercises usually involve methods that partners can use to circulate the breath and energy in their bodies. This book shows how partners can include fundamental consciousness in their sexual practice, to reach an even deeper level of contact with each other, and to facilitate the most profound level of spiritual realization.

There are exercises at the end of each of the following chapters so you can practice relating with other people in the dimension of spiritual oneness. They include ways for partners to directly experience the clear, unified space of fundamental consciousness; to contact each other from the core of their bodies; to experience the continuity of love, awareness and physical sensation; and to refine their senses so that they can see, hear and touch each other on a more subtle level. There are also exercises that combine traditional Tantric energy exercises with attunement to fundamental consciousness during sexual union.

These exercises are from *Subtle Self Work*®, a method that I have developed over the past twenty-five years. Unlike most traditional spiritual techniques, Subtle Self Work focuses directly both on awakening spiritual essence in our whole body, and on relating with other people while remaining in this essence.

Traditionally, spiritual transformation has been taught as a solitary practice, even requiring the avoidance of social attachments and commitments. This book views the true meaning of spiritual detachment as being the ability to allow life to flow without manipulation or defense. This means that we need to be fully open and available in our reception and response to life. Since our defensive strategies and rigidities were formed in relationship to other people, relationships are the ideal context for releasing those defenses.

If we do not include relationships in our spiritual practice, we often lose the realization we have gained as soon as we encounter another human being. But if we have practiced relating with other people in fundamental consciousness, we can maintain our spiritual realization in our daily lives, so that it is not a temporary peak experience, but a lasting transformation of consciousness.

Fundamental consciousness is a relational field, a unity of self and other. When we attempt to shut out either our environment or our internal life, we fragment our own consciousness, and this immediately conceals our essence. Spiritual oneness is the absolute balance of inward and outward contact. It is the deepest contact we can have with our own self and with everyone and everything that we encounter. It means that we are able to see through the surface of people and things to their essence. When we touch a plant or an animal or another human being, we can feel the streaming of the life force and the responsiveness of the subtle intelligence and love within them. We can experience that our own essence of sensation, love and awareness resonates with the same essential qualities of everything around us.

In the dimension of fundamental consciousness, intimate partners begin to know each other, to experience each other, through the whole internal depth of their being. This is immensely satisfying, because it is the object of our driving hunger for contact with other life. This contact – the ability to feel genuine love for another person, to experience the mental excitement of two minds meeting and the pleasure of unguarded physical sensation – is among the greatest rewards of spiritual awakening.

Judith Blackstone
Woodstock, NY

CHAPTER ONE
The Relational Field

FUNDAMENTAL CONSCIOUSNESS

The oneness of the spiritual dimension is the underlying reality of all relationships. It can be described as a relational field, a fundamental continuity of self and other. In the spaciousness and stillness of our spiritual essence, we are truly in contact, truly intimate, with ourselves and with all other life.

The idea that people are interconnected in a relational field is in agreement with the prevailing modern view of the world as an open 'system' in which all of the parts influence each other. In the field of psychology, the psychoanalytic theory of 'intersubjectivity' describes relationships as interactions of differently organized subjective worlds[1]. The relational field described in this book, however, is not made solely of inter-acting subjectivities. The intersubjective field is seen here as arising out of a more primary, unified field of fundamental consciousness. According to the Eastern spiritual teachings, the nature of this dimension is being, luminosity and bliss.

The spiritual essence of life is beyond our subjective ability to modify experience. To the extent that we are either consciously or unconsciously manipulating ourselves and our relationship with the world, we do not experience our funda-mental oneness with other people. Spiritual realization can be understood as the gradual transformation of the inter-subjective field of experience into the underlying relational field of spiritual oneness.

---

1   Robert D. Stolorow, George E. Atwood, *Contexts of Being* (Hillsdale, NJ: The Analytic Press, 1992)

Fundamental consciousness is the dimension of ultimate reality. It is an absolute unity between ourselves and other life. The various schools of Eastern spiritual philosophy have different ways of describing ultimate reality, but they point to the same experience of unity. For example, Sankara, the revered teacher of Hindu nondualism writes, 'I fill all things, inside and out, like space. Changeless and the same in all, I am pure, unattached, stainless and immutable.'[2]

A Buddhist text, from the Dzog-chen tradition, says, 'A direct awareness, sharp and awake. Possessing no existence, it is empty and pure, a clear openness of nondual luminosity and emptiness.'[3] Spiritual realization is a process of laying bare this underlying reality. It is a process of dissolving the subjective limitations and distortions of our essential being.

However, the Eastern spiritual traditions also teach that the complete realization of fundamental consciousness is extremely rare. In fact it may be that no one is completely realized, that the nature of embodied existence is always, to some extent, limited and subjective. But it is also clear, from observing the progression of spiritual realization, that we mature in the direction of ultimate reality.

Although absolute oneness is virtually unattainable in its entirety, it is not hypothetical. It is a dimension of ourselves that is unmistakable once we attune to it. It is an experiential and observable reality. It is a dimension of consciousness that transcends – that releases the constraints of – our own subjectivity. This is not a negation of our humanness. The experience of existing as a human being, of being alive to ourselves and the world around us, of responding to life with insight, emotion and sensation, increases as we release our subjective organization. As we realize this undistorted, unified consciousness, we have a sense of becoming real, and of experiencing life as it really is. When two people are both attuned to this dimension they have a sense of being in genuine contact with each other.

The image of a relational field also represents the spatial nature of fundamental consciousness. This dimension of existence is experienced as vast, empty space pervading everything, even physical space itself. When we attune to it we feel that we are made of empty space, and we feel continuous with the empty space that everything else is made of. This is an actual change in the texture of our experience. Instead of feeling solid and separate, we feel permeable, and everything around us also appears to be permeable.

People often ask me what sort of experience this is. Is it a sensation, a feeling, an awareness? Fundamental consciousness is the essence of our whole being and it is known through our whole being. It is an integration – the integrative ground – of awareness, sensation and emotion. Fundamental consciousness is said to be 'self-reflecting' because it awakens to itself. It knows itself. This type of knowing is unlike any other, for it is not an experience 'of' something in the same way that we have an experience of a blue sky, or of a feeling of sadness, or of a sensation of heat. Fundamental consciousness is the knower itself, not an object of the knower. To experience fundamental consciousness means that the knower begins to know itself.

When two people are both attuned to the relational field, they feel continuous with each other as being the empty space of fundamental consciousness. They experience that they are living in an unbounded field of unified presence. The nature of the spiritual dimension is bliss. Bliss is inherent in the space itself, and suffuses every aspect of their contact with each other.

CONSCIOUSNESS AND FLOW

Although the spiritual dimension of life is experienced as motionless space, all of the content of experience is movement. Feelings move, thoughts move, our physiological systems all move, even circumstances move. We experience the stillness of fundamental consciousness and the dynamic flow of life at the same time. The more we attune to, and become, the stillness, the more the movement of life occurs without obstruction, without resistance or distortion. The content of experience is inseparable from the stillness of fundamental consciousness, in the same way that waves are inseparable from the ocean. Everything that we experience in the spiritual dimension appears to be made of the same subtle consciousness that experiences it.

Zen Buddhism describes the unobstructed movement of life as 'leaving no trace'. It passes through the stillness of our consciousness without our grasping or manipulating it, and without disturbing or altering the stillness in any way. For example, if we feel sad and we do not interfere with this feeling at all, it will register vividly in our consciousness and then dissipate. But if we try not to feel sad, we will have to clamp down on the spontaneous movement of experience by constricting our body and energy system, and this will actually maintain the experience of sadness within our organism. If we continue to prevent this emotion from moving, the holding pattern will become a chronic rigidity in our being and any rigidity in our own being is also a barrier between ourselves and other people. It will also color our experience, so that life always seems a little sad. This is why spiritual realization requires that we accept and experience life just as it is, in each moment.

To the extent that two people are both attuned to the

stillness of fundamental consciousness, the exchange between them moves with fluidity and spontaneity. In this clear, unified space, it becomes easier to recognize and dissolve the residual barriers of numbness, fear, confusion and anger that separate us from other people, and impede this flow. Wherever the flow of exchange between partners gets 'stuck', that is where the healing can take place that will help both people open to their spiritual essence.

The unity of self and other is our true nature. Once we have reached this dimension of ourselves, we experience unity even with people who have not realized fundamental consciousness. We experience that our own essence is continuous with theirs – that the spaciousness that pervades our own being also pervades them. And we can still allow our own responses to flow freely and spontaneously. Many people fear that they will be lonely if they attune more subtly to life than the people around them. But this subtle attunement gives us a felt sense of kinship and connection with all other life.

THE BODY OF CLEAR SPACE

We cannot truly understand human development, or the dimension of spiritual oneness, unless we understand how the body is involved in the process of spiritual realization. The body can be experienced as physical matter, as energy or as consciousness. Our most subtle and clear experience of the body is that it is made of consciousness. This is the integration of body, energy and mind. Although the total unity of body and mind is considered a very advanced and rare attainment[4], we progress towards this integration as we realize funda-mental consciousness.

4 Lama Thubten Yeshe writes, 'With achievement of the illusory body, a very high attainment, there is total unity of body and mind.' *The Bliss of Inner Fire* (Boston, MA: Wisdom Publications, 1998), p.84

Our experience of spiritual oneness is obstructed by static areas in our body and energy system. These are places within our organism that we are literally holding still against the flow of experience. Some of these patterns are chronic, the tissues of the body having rigidified in the shape of the holding pattern, while others are evoked by specific circumstances that remind us of painful events in our past. But they are all somatic patterns; they are organizations of our whole organism. These holding patterns impede and distort our contact with ourselves and with other people. They diminish our awareness, emotion and sensation and they also limit our physiological functioning.

The aspect of our consciousness that organizes these patterns is called the 'causal consciousness'. In the traditional spiritual literature it is considered to be one of the 'sheaths', or subtle bodies, pervading our whole individual form. Another name for it is *buddhi*. It is also said to be the aspect of ourselves that realizes fundamental consciousness. As we let go of our holding patterns, our causal consciousness becomes one with fundamental consciousness.

As I will explain more fully in the next chapter, spiritual realization is not just a return to the non-defended state of infancy. However, we do need to let go of our holding patterns in order for the process of human development to continue towards spiritual maturity. When we live in the dimension of fundamental consciousness, we are able to experience these held areas in our body as tensions within the fluidity of our experience, or as densities within the clear space of our consciousness. Some people describe seeing them as patches of darkness within the luminosity of the spiritual dimension.

As we become one with the relational field of fundamental consciousness, the physical body becomes less rigid, less held in position. We have a sense of inhabiting the internal space of our body, of reclaiming the space that we had constricted in our defensive organizations. And we gain depth, range and authenticity in our contact with the world around us.

Our somatic holding patterns are connected with static beliefs and repetitive behaviors. This can be illustrated by a woman named Sara who came to work with me because she seemed unable to maintain an intimate relationship. She was extremely lonely and, as she was now in her late forties, she had begun to despair that she would never find love. She told me that men always ended relationships with her just when she was beginning to feel really involved with them. When we met Sara had just started going out with someone new, and she was afraid that the same pattern would repeat again.

When Sara described her isolation to me, I was surprised. She seemed to me a very warm, lively and trusting woman. As she sat across from me I could feel the movement of love in the space between us. However, each time she mentioned one of the men she had known, the same shift occurred in her. There was a hardening deep inside her chest and at the same time in her eyes and her brow. There was also a subtle upward displacement of her energy, so that her forehead became the dominant location of her presence, conveying a sense of superiority and judgement. This holding pattern stopped the flow of love in our relational field, just as it had in her relationships with men.

Sara herself was unaware of the shift that had taken place in her, so she was always confused and surprised when men responded to it with their own defenses and, in the end, by leaving her. When I pointed it out to her, however, she could feel it in her body, and she recognized it as a familiar movement. With a little practice she could shift in and out of the holding pattern as a voluntary movement. I asked her to shift into it as she pictured one of the men from her past.

When she did this she recognized that she was trying not to love him. When she pictured the same man and released the holding pattern, she felt longing for him, and then fear that he would reject her, and then grief that the relationship had ended.

As she allowed herself to feel this pain, she remembered that her father had suddenly become withdrawn from her when she was about five years old. He was often not home in the evenings, as he had been before, and when he was home he seemed less affectionate towards her. Sara also remembered that her mother was very critical of her father at around this same time. She could picture her mother scolding her father as if he were a child, while he withdrew into stony silence. In order to cope with the heartache of her father's withdrawal, she had shut down her own loving response towards him and, at the same time, she had imitated her mother's critical attitude. This imitation of attitude, which psychologists call 'introjection', is an unconscious mirroring of our parent's (or caretaker's) subjective organization. It is not just an imitation of behavior, but of the subjective organization of the whole organism.

I then asked Sara to imagine her father in front of her, and she was able to observe that she automatically closed her heart as she pictured him. As she released this holding pattern, she was able to feel her deep grief at the loss of his love. After this session Sara practiced keeping her heart open in her relationship with the new man in her life. Although she still went into her familiar holding pattern at times, she could recognize the shift as it occurred and release it. She also understood that this holding pattern signaled that she was feeling vulnerable because she was feeling love.

The shifts in the organization of our body and energy system are usually so subtle that they go unnoticed. When therapists work with couples it is important that they watch specifically for where the relational field is open or closed between the partners, and how this changes as they discuss their relationship. Working with individuals, these same shifts occur in the relational field with the therapist, as the person describes their current difficulties and the important events of their past. This subtle 'dance of veils' is the key to understanding the problematic areas of a person's life, and to helping them open to their spiritual essence.

THE AUTHENTIC SELF

We realize the dimension of spiritual oneness through subtle, inward attunement to our own body. Even if the focus of our spiritual practice is outside of our body, we cannot realize the essence of life without realizing the essence of our own being, which is unified and continuous with it. It is a paradox of nature that the more inward contact we have with our own form, the more we experience oneness with other life. This means that the transcendence (the openness) of our individual form and the inhabiting of our individual form occur at the same time. Our individual wholeness and our oneness with other life develop simultaneously, through the realization of fundamental consciousness.

As the barriers between ourselves and other people dissolve, we are able to feel more whole and intact within our own being. We experience an internal continuity of spiritual essence that seems to collect and 'jell' within our body as our realization progresses. We can rest in our essence without having to support it in any way. We feel both intact within ourselves and yet entirely permeable, entirely continuous with our environment. It requires no effort at all to live within our own body.

Spiritual realization is therefore synonymous with personal maturity. As we inhabit the internal space of our body, we awaken the inherent capacities of our being. For example, we develop our capacity for love, understanding and physical pleasure, as well as the most subtle and accurate functioning of all our senses.

In Hindu nondual (Advaita) philosophy, fundamental consciousness is described as the one, unified consciousness of the universe – a single self that is experienced as the primary self of all beings. This is similar to the Jewish mystical conception, which says that we are all sparks of a single flame, that we are all embodiments of a single light, a single source of wisdom and love.

In Hindu philosophy, one of the names of fundamental consciousness is 'Self'. As I have said, this refers to the single self of all creation. But this term is not just a concept; it is also a qualitative description of our essence. We can enter the dimension of fundamental consciousness through attunement to the quality of self within the internal space of our body. Although it is difficult to describe this quality, I have found that when I ask people to attune to the quality of self, most of them have no difficulty doing it.

You can test this out quickly yourself, if you wish, by taking a moment to feel that you inhabit the internal space of your arms. Now attune to the quality of your self inside your arms. Although this is not a quality that we usually notice, because it is the ground of life and not the content, it has always been there, as part of the feeling of being alive. To attune to it is like finding the most slender thread of gold in a complex tapestry.

Some people object to the word 'self' in this context because it can easily be confused with the constructed self – the subjective organization of oneself – that conceals the reality of spiritual oneness. They suggest that I use the word 'being'. Interestingly, however, attunement to being does not bring us into as subtle a dimension of ourselves as attunement to self. Attuning to the quality of self evokes the spiritual dimension within the internal space of the body, and the dissolution of the barriers between internal and external experience. And attuning to the quality of self within just one part of the body, for example, our arms, brings us into the spiritual dimension within our entire body.

Attunement to the quality of self is an exercise, or practice. The realization of our spiritual essence is a relaxed state; in fact, it is our most relaxed, natural state, not an action of any sort. But the exercise functions like a stretch for our consciousness, that eventually enables us to settle into this most subtle dimension of ourselves without any effort.

The quality of self is not the same as our many ideas about ourselves that make up what we might call our 'false identity'. These are static images of ourselves – for example the image of authority, or the image of cheerfulness – that we have assumed to cope with the challenges of our particular life circumstances. They are part of our defensive holding pattern: subjective organizations that stop the flow of experience and obstruct our contact with our essence. Over time, these images harden within the tissues of the body, forming rigid personae which we can easily mistake for our true being. The singer, Paul Simon, describes these self-images vividly in his album *Graceland* when he says that he doesn't want to become a 'cartoon in a cartoon world'. It can be difficult to recognize, or to give up, these false images because they are often effective. Once other people are convinced by our persona, our interactions with them constantly augment our false character structure. Then we feel locked into relationships that seem to require us to always be that cartoon of authority, or that smiling 'happy face'.

The authenticity of the self that occurs with spiritual realization is not just a shift in the way we experience ourselves. It can also be observed by other people as a transformation of the way we look and sound, even of the quality of our touch. Although I have witnessed this transformation many times, it still seems to me as mysterious and amazing an aspect of nature as birth or death.

For example, a man named Leo had been coming to work with me for about five months. I did not know much about him. Although he was always warm and cordial, he did not talk about himself, but liked to get right to the meditation exercises. He came in and sat down, closed his eyes, and I lead him through the Subtle Self Work. Then he opened his eyes, and sometimes asked me a question about the work, or reported on some new experience that he had had that session, and got up and left. Over the months I watched him deepen, as if he were gradually materializing within his body. Then one day, when he opened his eyes, there he was, looking out at me. It was an unmistakable shift, from the polite, veiled expression that he always wore, to the unmasked, vital presence of a real person. I could see him, and though I still did not know many details about his life, I knew him.

Because our essence pervades our whole body, to become attuned to it means that we become alive throughout the whole internal depth of ourselves. In his novel *Fup*, Jim Dodge has a character say, "If you just stand still and *feel* for a moment you would know how everything yearns to be wild."[5] To live in the subtle, spiritual ground of ourselves is to arrive at our own wild existence.

We all have a natural ability to recognize authenticity. Just as we can tell balance from imbalance, or harmony from

---

5   Jim Dodge, *Fup* (Berkeley, CA: City Miner Books, 1983), p.44

dissonance, we are designed to detect the ring of truth. This capacity becomes increasingly acute as we realize fundamental consciousness. It is a navigational tool for guiding us towards the realization of our authentic, spiritual being. We also have a natural craving for authenticity. Although we may not know what we are missing, if we become too cut off from our real self, too ensnared in our false persona, we become depressed; life seems meaningless. This lack of meaning has been one of the major themes of the past century for philosophers, artists and psychologists. When we direct our focus inward, however, we discover that we are not the 'hollow men' that the poet, T.S. Eliot, described, but full of the natural power, love and intelligence of our true nature.

DISENTANGLEMENT AND SPONTANEITY

As we recognize ourselves as the stillness of spiritual oneness, all of our experience flows freely through us. Each moment of life registers with its full impact. We become disentangled from the flow of life, as we become more responsive to life. This is our most natural, relaxed condition. It is important that we do not try to hold our focus on either the stillness or the movement. To live in the dimension of spiritual oneness means that we do not hold onto any aspect of experience.

It is particularly challenging to allow life to flow in our intimate relationships, because this means that we cannot secure the source of our pleasure. To be one with another person requires that we accept the transient nature of life. Just as an acceptance of our own mortality can make life richer, however, and certainly does not make us any more mortal, the acceptance that we cannot control the flow of circumstances brings value and keen awareness to each moment.

Some people are afraid that to let go in this way means

that they will act on every destructive or lewd impulse that occurs in them. But fundamental consciousness is our dimension of wholeness. Although we do register all of our impulses in this dimension, our actions emerge from our whole being, including our mental clarity and compassion.

The awakening of spontaneity can be one of the most challenging aspects of spiritual realization. It may remind us of painful situations in our childhood when our hearts and minds were open and available, while the adults with whom we interacted were far more guarded. To allow ourselves to become truly responsive and authentic again, in a world that does not always return or honor those qualities, requires courage. We can base this courage on compassion for the confusion and suffering that is shared, in various degrees, by all human beings.

It is also important to understand that our true self, our spiritual essence, cannot be altered in any way. We can trust the absolute durability of our true nature. A Tibetan Buddhist teacher once told me that our true nature is 'harder than a rock'. In the Hindu literature it is said to be 'uncreated, unborn', and in Zen Buddhism they describe it as 'I have never moved from the beginning'.

Since fundamental consciousness is unchanged by the content of experience, it cannot be damaged. Although we can certainly feel emotional pain, our experience of essence is unchanged by it. Although we may feel that we have been severely damaged by circumstances in our past, once we reach the essence of ourselves, we know that we are essentially whole and well. None of our innate functions – our creativity, or our capacity to love or think or experience sexual pleasure, to name just a few – can be diminished by another person. We can only constrict our own attunement to these indestructible aspects of our own being.

The ability to relax, and allow ourselves to be as we are in each moment, also means that we can allow other people to be just as they are. One of the major challenges of intimate relationships is accepting the 'otherness' of another person. Many people protect themselves against the otherness of other people, because they fear that it will impinge on their own identity, that it will invade and curtail their own connection with themselves. But in the all-pervasive space of fundamental consciousness, there is plenty of room for one's own being and the being of another person. As we begin to live in this dimension, our inward attunement is no longer challenged by the otherness of another person. In the unchanging relational field of emptiness and bliss, we can experience the movement of another person's experience at the same time as we experience the movement of our own experience. We can then observe, with interest and curiosity, how the exchange between ourselves and another person unfolds. This means that we are able to get to truly know that person, and to interact with them. We do not have to make the relationship happen, we do not have to make it work in any particular way, for we see that the actual exchange between ourselves and another person unfolds to produce its own true form.

EXERCISE 1
ATTUNEMENT TO FUNDAMENTAL
CONSCIOUSNESS

The following is an exercise from Subtle Self Work for attuning to fundamental consciousness. It can be practiced alone. It is followed by an exercise that couples can practice together for relating with each other in this subtle dimension. Both of these exercises attune directly to the unified relational field. They are very effective 'stretches' that can help you eventually settle into this dimension without any effort. For best results, they should be followed by a short period of sitting without any object of focus.

The exercises are designed to evoke subtle experiences that may be unfamiliar to you. If the instructions seem obscure to you, allow yourself to respond to them without questioning their meaning. With practice, the intended experience will become clear, and understanding will follow from experience. You may find it helpful to make a tape of yourself reading the exercise so that you can practice it without looking at the book. Partners can also take turns reading the instructions to each other. The exercise usually takes about thirty-five minutes.

Sit with your back straight, either on a chair or cross-legged on a cushion on the floor. Close your eyes. Breathe smoothly and evenly, through your nostrils, throughout the whole exercise.

Bring your attention down to your feet. Feel that you are inside your feet, that you inhabit your feet. Now attune to the quality of your self, a particular quality that feels like your self, inside your feet. Make sure that you can stay in your feet as you breathe; that your inhale does not lift you up out of your feet.

Feel that you are inside your ankles and your lower legs. Attune to the quality of your self inside your ankles and your lower legs.

Feel that you are inside your knees. Now balance your awareness of the space inside your knees, find both these internal areas at the same time. Experience the absolute stillness of your balanced consciousness. (Fundamental consciousness is absolutely still because it is balanced.)

Feel that you are inside your thighs. Attune to the quality of your self inside your thighs.

Feel that you are inside your hip sockets. From the inside of your hip sockets, you can feel the internal space of your thighs, and the internal space of your pelvis at the same time. Balance your awareness of the space inside your hip sockets; find the inside of both hip sockets at the same time. Experience the stillness of your balanced consciousness and the movement of your breath at the same time. (These are two different aspects of yourself, experienced at the same time. Your consciousness is still and your breath is moving.)

Feel that you are inside your pelvis. Attune to the quality of your self inside your pelvis. Bring your breath down into your pelvis on your inhalation, and let it pass through the quality of your self inside your pelvis.

Feel that you are inside your mid-section, between your ribs and your pelvis, including the solar plexus area under the ribs. Attune to the quality of self, inside your mid-section. Bring your breath down into your mid-section, and let it pass through the quality of self inside your mid-section.

Feel that you are inside your chest. Attune to the quality of your self inside your chest. Bring your breath down into your chest and let it pass through the quality of self inside your chest.

Feel that you are inside your shoulders. Attune to the quality of your self inside your shoulders.

Feel that you are inside your shoulder sockets. From the inside of your shoulder sockets, you can feel the internal space of your upper arms, and the internal space of your chest at the same time.

Balance your awareness of the inside of your shoulder sockets; find the inside of both shoulder sockets at the same time. Feel the stillness of the balanced consciousness and the movement of your breath at the same time. The breath passes through the stillness of your consciousness.

Feel that you are inside your arms, wrists and hands, all the way to your fingertips. Attune to the quality of your self inside your arms, wrists and hands.

Feel that you are inside your neck. Attune to the quality of your self inside your neck. Bring your breath down through your neck and let it pass through the quality of self inside your neck.

Feel that you are inside your head. Feel that you are behind your whole forehead, inside your eyes, behind your cheekbones, inside your nose, mouth, jaw and chin. Keep breathing as you do this. Feel that you are inside your ears. Now feel that you are inside both hemispheres of your brain. Feel the quality of your self inside your whole brain. Let your breath be subtle enough to move through your head and let it pass through the quality of self inside your whole brain.

Now feel that you are inside your whole body all at once. Attune to the quality of the self in your whole body. Keep breathing smoothly through your nostrils as you do this.

Keeping your eyes closed, mentally find the space outside your body, the space in the room.

Experience that the space inside your body and the space outside your body is the same, continuous space; it pervades you. You are still inside your body, but your body is pervaded by space.

Now open your eyes, and again feel that you are inside your whole body all at once. Attune to the quality of self in your whole body. Mentally find the space outside your body. Feel that the space inside and outside of your body is the same, continuous space. It pervades you. This present moment is experienced inside and outside you at the same time.

Experience that the space pervading your body also pervades the other people and objects in the room. But you are still inside your whole body. Do not project yourself into the other people or objects in the room. You are attuning to the space that is already pervading you and them.

Experience that the space pervading your body also pervades the walls of the room. Remain inside your whole body while you experience the space pervading both your body and the walls of the room. Let go of any action of attunement and rest in the pervasive space of fundamental consciousness.

EXERCISE 2
ATTUNEMENT TO FUNDAMENTAL
CONSCIOUSNESS WITH A PARTNER

Sit facing your partner. Keep your eyes open. Breathe calmly and evenly through your nose. Experience that you are inside your whole body at once. Mentally find the space outside your body. Experience that the space inside and outside your body is the same continuous space.

Experience that the space pervading your own body also pervades your partner's body. Remain in your own body while you experience this. Again, do not project yourself into your partner's body. Attune to the space that is already pervading you and your partner. Let your breath pass through the space of your own body, on both your inhale and your exhale. (You are breathing your own location in space.) Practice allowing yourself and your partner to just be in the space, continuous with each other but not merged.

Let your eyes relax. Your eyes are also pervaded by space; they are made of space. Experience that you are seeing each other with the space itself – the space does the seeing. The space sees both you and your partner at the same time. Let go of any action of attunement and rest in the pervasive space of fundamental consciousness.

If you do not have a partner, you can practice this exercise in any group of people; for example, in a restaurant or a theater. Experience that the space that pervades your own body also pervades the other people. Remain inside your own body as you do this, and let your breath pass through the space inside your own body. Practice allowing yourself and the other people to be just as they are, in the space.

CHAPTER TWO

Oneness and Separateness

THE DEVELOPMENT OF THE RELATIONAL FIELD

When Charles and Miriam came to work with me, they had been married for a year and a half. Although they were having difficulty adjusting to living together, the love between them was obvious. If either of them became upset as they spoke, the other would watch with anguish, and then reach over to pat and caress. When the first session was over, they handled the details of payment and setting the next appointment with a cozy, secure togetherness. So I was almost as shocked as Charles when Miriam announced, during their second session, that she had decided to get her own apartment.

'I used to read books,' she said, gesturing towards my bookcases. 'I could think! My favorite activity was sitting with a book on philosophy or psychology and making notes in my journal. Now my favorite activity is lying in our bedroom in front of the TV with Charlie, eating nachos.' 'You don't have to do that', Charles protested. 'I can watch TV by myself, and you could go think in the living room.' 'No, I can't,' she answered. 'There are plenty of afternoons when I get home and you're still at work. But I just don't get any thoughts anymore.' She turned to me, 'It's like I don't exist the way I used to. All I can feel is Charlie.'

As she began to cry, Charles moved towards her and put his arm around her shoulders. Miriam leaned her head against his chest, and a strange thing happened. Her strength seemed to drain out of her; her intelligent presence became dim and diffuse. Still leaning against him, she turned her face to me and smiled weakly, and it was really as if she no longer existed; some vital part of her being had departed.

THE BOUNDARY PROBLEM IN RELATIONSHIPS

One of the most common problems that people have in intimate relationships is that they feel lost or submerged in the other person, or they fear that this will happen if they allow themselves to be truly intimate. Some people cope with this fear by distancing themselves from other people, by closing themselves off to external influence, or finding ways to push people away. Others cope in a seemingly opposite way, by attempting to merge with the identity of their partner. Most of us do some of both. These relational styles are ways of accommodating the defensive barrier that we have created, early in our lives, between ourselves and other people. They are a continuation of the delicate negotiation, which begins in infancy and can last our whole lives, between connection with ourselves and connection with other people. This quandary of choice between self-love and love for others is, at root, illusory, for we are fundamentally whole within our own being and one with other people, at the same time. Love is an essential quality of the whole field.

The fear of losing one's own identity in relationships is so central to the challenge of being intimate with another person that I could find some expression of it in any of the couples who come to work with me. To some extent, the fear of identity loss is the fear of ego loss. In an intimate relationship our ideas about ourselves, and our strategies for getting approval, maintaining one-upmanship and so forth, are always challenged. There is almost always some conflict between our partner's intimate view of us and the image that we are trying to project. These conflicts can be very helpful for dismantling our holding patterns. I have found however, that the reason so many people are unable to surrender their defenses in relationships is that they are defending something even more precious to them than their constructed ego. They are protecting their actual connection with themselves – their self-enjoyment.

Since the experience of self-connection is difficult to define, the loss of it is often expressed as a vague but intolerable malaise. It is described as a loss of 'space', a sense of being 'out of sync' with oneself. People may speak of feeling cut off from their own needs and desires, or from their own thoughts and feelings. Some people feel as if they are seeing the world through their partner's eyes, that they can no longer connect with their own perceptions and responses. The loss of self-connection is experienced as a breach of boundaries, an inability to juggle the guarding of one's own parameters with the openness of intimacy. The perceived threat of intrusion often gives rise to power struggles, turning the act of mutual decision-making into a fight to the death.

The loss of self-connection comes from the inability to attune inward to the source of our own experience, within the internal space of our body. Our awareness of our partner overwhelms and replaces our contact with ourselves. However, instead of feeling a connection with that person, we feel bound up in them.

In my last book, *The Enlightenment Process*, I quote R. D. Laing's description of the loss of self-connection.

'If the individual does not feel himself to be autonomous this means that he can experience neither his separateness from, nor his relatedness to, the other in the usual way. A lack of sense of autonomy implies that one feels one's being bound up in the other, or that the other is bound up in oneself, in a sense that transgresses the actual possibilities within the structure of human relatedness. It means that a feeling that one is in a position of ontological dependency on the other (i.e., dependent on the other for one's very being), is substituted for a sense of relatedness and attachment to him based on genuine mutuality.'[6]

This common difficulty in relationships can be particularly confusing and troublesome for people who are interested in spiritual transformation. Since spiritual realization is the unity of oneself and everything else, they ask, shouldn't we surrender our connection with ourselves? And isn't the resentment that one feels at being overwhelmed by another person's presence, simply one's own clinging to the illusion of existing separately from that person?

In order to progress on the spiritual path, it is important to understand the difference between lack of self-contact and the dissolution of ego. In order to realize true oneness with other people we need to understand the difference between spiritual unity and the experience of being 'bound up' in another person that R.D. Laing describes.

THE EQUALITY OF FUNDAMENTAL CONSCIOUSNESS

As I described in the last chapter, we experience the unified spiritual dimension of life as vast space, pervading all of the various forms of life equally. This experience is sometimes called nonduality, or 'one taste'. It is important to understand that this unified existence is not something outside of ourselves. It includes ourselves. Our own being is the same 'one taste' as everything around us. This is our most relaxed state. The

---

6   R.D. Laing, *The Divided Self* (Tavistock, 1959; Baltimore, MD: Penguin, 1965), pp.52-53, quoted in Judith Blackstone, *The Enlightenment Process* (Boston, MA: Element, 1997), pp.75-76

Tibetan Buddhists call it 'natural mind' or 'primordial awareness'.

As we let go of our defensive holding patterns, we relax into the unified dimension of existence. This feels as if we are dissolving in space, becoming more and more permeable, or translucent. At the same time, it feels as if we are truly existing, as if we are being born. It feels as if we are coming into contact with parts of ourselves, actual places within our body, that have been numb and unavailable; as if we are becoming whole within the internal space of our body. This is an emptiness of defensive structures and a fullness of our essential being. Spiritual oneness is not an experience of submerging our own existence in the existence of another person. It is not a diffusion of our own sense of being outward into the environment. It is a deepened and simultaneous contact with ourselves and our environment.

Interestingly, however, spiritual oneness is not a return to the non-defended condition of infancy. According to the observations of developmental psychologists, we begin life with just a rudimentary ability for self-contact and connection with other people. Early childhood development is described as the increasing ability to differentiate between ourselves and our environment, to recognize and express our own needs and perceptions and, at the same time, as an increasing ability to connect with other people. Although children are as unguarded as spiritually realized adults, they have just begun the process of inward contact and connection with others.

A MODEL OF HUMAN DEVELOPMENT

In the past two decades, psychologists have emphasized that childhood development always occurs in relationship with other people. From the beginning of our lives, we exist in a relational field with our environment. I suggest that the realization of spiritual oneness is a continuation of the child's budding experience of the self/other relational field.

I believe that we can view all human growth, from childhood to spiritual maturity, as the gradual realization of the essential unity of the relational field. The child's initial inward contact comes to fruition as the internal wholeness of spiritual realization. And the child's initial connection with the environment matures into the spiritual oneness, the absolute unity, of self and other. It is this process that engenders our defensive holding patterns and it is this same process that continues to unfold as we release those holding patterns.

We can see from this that there is more to spiritual realization than letting go of our psychological defenses. This letting go, or dissolving, of egoic structures only allows the process of human development to continue. The actual process of development is still a mystery, and it appears to be innate – a natural function. There appears to be a spontaneous movement towards increasing contact with the self/other relational field that drives the child's process of development, and which continues to unfold in adulthood as we let go of our defensive grip on ourselves. Just as a tree needs the appropriate environmental conditions to grow from its seed, human beings need the appropriate conditions for this developmental process. Just as the tree, and all of its basic characteristics, can be predicted from the seed, so spiritual realization, having the same basic characteristics universally, is the predictable outcome of human development.

The movement of human development proceeds through deeper levels of contact with ourselves and our environment. This deepening contact brings us into increasingly subtle and unified realms of existence, or increasingly subtle attunement to ourselves and the world around us. This process of deepening arrives finally at the spiritual dimension of unified, fundamental consciousness, but there is still much further to go. When we reach the experience of 'one taste', we have just begun the most advanced phase of human development. As I will explain more fully in a later chapter, we can continue to 'fill out' our realization of spiritual oneness for the rest of our lives. If we look at the advanced spiritual practices that accompany the world's most profound metaphysical philosophies, we will see that they are all designed to help us either loosen our defensive grip on ourselves or attune directly to the innermost core of our being and the most subtle dimension of consciousness. In other words, they are designed to accelerate the innate process of human development.

NEUROSIS AS A SCHISM IN THE FIELD OF ONENESS

According to developmental psychologists such as Margaret Mahler and Daniel Stern, children gradually deepen their connection with themselves as individuals distinct from their environment. Mahler claims that we begin life in a state of merged identity with our primary caregiver, and then proceed through what she calls the 'separation-individuation sequence'[7]. Stern says that there is always some amount of self-distinction, even in infants, but that this increases over time. He also says that this deepening self-connection occurs simultaneously with the ability to connect with other people[8]. But both agree that the direction of childhood development is towards the recognition of self and other.

I describe this developing recognition of self and other as 'spatial' because it produces a deepening of perspective on life. At first, we can barely distinguish our own self from the

7 Margaret Mahler, *The Psychological Birth of the Human Infant* (New York: Bantam Books, 1975)
8 Daniel N. Stern, *The Interpersonal World of the Infant* (New York: Basic Books, 1985)

people who hold and nurture us. Then we begin to discover our own sensations, emotions, perceptions and needs, as belonging to our own being. At the same time, we begin to recognize, respond to and communicate with people who are other than our own being. This is a deepening of perspective, a polarization of self and other.

When someone holds us, for example, we can sense that our own body is separate from their body. We begin to notice that the emotions of other people are different from our own; that we can feel sadness, for example as someone else feels happy or angry. As we continue to deepen our experience of ourselves, we also begin to have an understanding of what is going on around us, and we form opinions, ideas and beliefs. Through the use of our developing verbal ability, we learn that our thoughts differ from those of other people; agreement and argument become possible. We become increasingly separate from other people, but because we are separate, we are able to touch them, to feel love and other emotions for them, and to communicate verbally with them. Inward contact gives us distance from our surroundings. At the same time, it develops our relational capacities, such as understanding, emotion and physical sensation.

We reach our deepest perspective when we contact the subtle channel that runs through the vertical core of our body. It is called *sushumna* in the Hindu yoga system and 'the central channel' in Tibetan Buddhism. This is our deepest connection with our own being; it is in every way the core of our being. At the same time it is our entranceway into fundamental consciousness, the dimension of our oneness with everything around us. When we contact the core of our body, we reach our deepest perspective on life; people and objects actually seem further away. At the same time, we experience the absolute oneness of the internal space of our own form with the internal space of everything around us.

Thus human development continues to unfold, under favorable conditions, towards spiritual maturity. As it turns out, however, this process is so fraught with difficulty and obstruction that it tends to become arrested or, at best, economized, in virtually every human life. By economized I mean that some aspects of ourselves become developed and others do not. Because the process of deepening self-contact and connection with others is not accomplished in isolation, but in relationship with other people, it is greatly influenced by the capacity of those other people for self-contact and connection. In other words, it is difficult for us, as children, to become more distinct from our parents than they are from us, or to be more connected with our parents than they are with us. The developmental process of developing contact with both ourselves and others must accommodate our specific family legacy of developmental arrest and economy. Our beginning realization of the unified relational field must accommodate the size and shape – perspective and economy – of our family.

In attempting to both separate from and connect with our mother, for example, we will have to accommodate her own history of loss, abandonment or rejection; her fear of connection, or anger at separation; her defenses that limit the depth of her sensation, love and awareness, as well as her unconscious strategies for avoiding pain. And all of this accommodation and adjustment will occur in a complex economy in which some types of connection (emotional, physical or mental) are available while others are obstructed.

As we navigate this particular relationship, we will both imitate her defenses and strategies and form our own. We will learn just how much and what kind of contact we can have with ourselves without loss of her love, and just how much and what kind of connection we can have with her without loss of our selves. We will make some compromises, trading a bit of self-contact for the sake of connection with her – or at least some semblance of connection, for true connection with others requires self-contact. We will also endure a degree of alienation from her for the sake of contact with our own sensations, feelings and thoughts. But again, the contact we have with ourselves will be limited by our defense against connection with her, for all our defenses limit the relational field as a whole. Our defenses limit our self-contact and our connection with others equally. We cannot close our heart to someone else without closing our heart.

The constraints, attitudes and strategies that we develop for both protecting our self-contact and for assuring our connection with other people, harden with repeated use into habitual ways of being. In this way, our pattern of openness and defense, our degree of authenticity and distortion, our ability to trust the flow of exchange between ourselves and others or our need to manipulate it, are all formed in relationship to the people we encounter first in our lives. Likewise, our ability to enjoy solitude, to notice our true desires and needs, to create or to think for ourselves, is formed within the context of these relationships.

Some of the defensive holding patterns that we form in these relationships become bound in the physical tissues of our body, constricting even our physical form. Other patterns emerge in response to circumstances that remind us of difficult situations in our past. All of these formations diminish the functions and capacities of our being. For example, with our own protective grip on ourselves, we limit our capacity for love and sensation. We constrict our senses. We restrain our voice and our creativity. We pull away from the support of the ground. We grip the muscles that we need in order to reach out or to embrace, or to take in nourishment.

These rigidities hold us in the perspective and economy of our childhood relational field. It is this defended relational field that we bring to our present relationships. Within the limitations of this field, we continue to negotiate the boundaries of self and other, and to balance self-contact with connection to others. In each new relationship we confront the same riddle of how open we can be with this person without loss of our own self, and to what extent we can be who we really are without loss of their love.

MERGING AND DISTANCING

Our defensive patterns both contract and fragment the relational field. They form a defensive barrier between ourselves and our environment. At the same time, they hold us in our childhood perspective on life – in our childhood sphere of self and other. They hold us in the unresolved conflicts of our childhood, in the deficits of contact, and the arrested flow of unexpressed responses. The defenses that were meant to protect us from the world actually keep us bound up in it, unable to get the distance, the inward contact, that we need in order to connect.

In this contracted, fragmented relational field, we feel both too close to other people and alienated from them at the same time. We feel encroached upon at the same time as we feel unable to truly connect. We cope with this predicament by both distancing ourselves from others and by attempting to merge with them.

These two relational styles are not just sets of behaviors; they involve the placement of our attention in the relational field. People who mainly distance themselves from other people have trained their attention on themselves and attempted to ignore, or at least filter, the vivid presence of others. Since their defenses prevent them from actual contact with their own being, they seem to reside mostly in their thinking minds, or their imagination, which sometimes gives them an air of abstraction or preoccupation. These people actually seem distant, as if they have a moat around them. But they are not really distant. They usually feel that life impinges on them with devastating force, and that they must defend against it at all cost. To the best of their abilities, they are protecting their precious contact with themselves.

People who abandon their self-contact for the sake of connection place their attention more on other people than on themselves. When we relate with a person who is merging, we feel that they are too close to us, that they are in our 'space'. People who merge with others usually think of themselves as being very loving, very concerned for other people. And they have made a great sacrifice in order to feel connected with people. But because their inward contact is diminished, they cannot truly make the connection that they seek.

So both of these strategies for coping with the defended boundary between ourselves and other people are ineffective and unsatisfying. The self that we defend in isolation is just a shadow of our true self. And the connection that we make by attempting to merge with other people is just a fraction of our capacity for intimacy. It is through inward contact with our own organism that we become capable of true contact with other people. We grow towards our true distance from other people and our true oneness with them at the same time.

I first noticed this about twenty years ago, while I was living at a Zen monastery in upstate New York. It is an old joke that the hardest thing about being a monk is other monks and, although I was not technically a monk, this was particularly true for me. I arrived at the monastery at a very low point in my life. I had suffered some losses several years before and had been living in near isolation ever since. I found the communal situations of monastic life almost unbearable; the hardy presence of other souls bruising and disruptive. We were expected to eat all our meals together, to work together cleaning the monastery, and to socialize together on the two days each week when the formal schedule was suspended. We also meditated together twice a day, sitting in silence and absolute stillness, attending to our breath or to the compelling phrase of a Zen koan.

It was in this stillness that I first noticed the movement inward: how each breath brought me infinitesimally closer to the core of my body. As the year went by, and this inward movement progressed, I began to notice that I felt further away from the people around me. I could look across the distance and connect with them. I could feel their presence while still feeling my own. I could feel the stillness that was the same in all of us, that was continuous between us, and that was unchanged by even the most boisterous movement of thoughts, feelings and sensations.

It is very interesting that when we inhabit the internal space of our body, the barrier between ourselves and other people dissolves. We experience the internal wholeness of our own form and the environment as continuous space. But when we live on the surface of ourselves, as most people do, we live in divided space; we feel separate from everything around us. We can say that the world of the severely defended person is 'almost' flat, whereas, at the other end of the spectrum, the world of the advanced spiritual master is 'almost' round. This is a deepening of perspective; a deepening of contact with self and other.

CONCLUSION

When we relate with another person in the dimension of spiritual oneness, we do not lose our essential identity. We experience that we are one essence, without losing our own embodiment of essence. When we shake hands with another person in this dimension, we experience that our own hand is continuous with the hand of the other person. As fundamental consciousness, there is no separation between our own hand and the other person's hand. At the same time, how-ever, we know our own being in our own hand, and the other person's being in the hand that we shake. The recognition of self and other is reflected in the clear, unified space of fundamental consciousness.

And whatever communication occurs between our own hand and the other person's hand is also clearly reflected in this space, in this unified relational field of consciousness of the two hands. One person may communicate love, for example, while the other communicates respect. The subtle currents of this communication move freely in the unob-structed space, producing a dance of intermingled currents, an excitement of interference patterns, that is transmitted throughout the energy systems of both people. And at the same time, as fundamental consciousness, we each discern our own communication from the communication of the other person. This is the paradox of spiritual oneness: we are each whole within ourselves and unified with everything else at the same time.

EXERCISE 3 – INHABITING THE BODY

In this exercise, partners help each other contact and inhabit the internal space of the body.

Partner A sits upright on a chair.

Partner B stands behind the chair and puts his or her hands on either side of Partner A's head.

Partner A inhabits the space between Partner B's hands.

Partner B may be able to feel when Partner A inhabits the space between his or her hands. The space will feel alive with Partner A's presence.

Then repeat the exercise, changing roles.

This exercise can be practiced with any part of the body. For example, Partner B can put his or her hands on either side of Partner A's shoulder or leg or wrist, helping Partner A inhabit that space.

CHAPTER THREE

Dancing Core-to-Core

OUR DEEPEST PERSPECTIVE

When we deepen our perspective from the periphery of ourselves to the innermost core of our being, we enter into fundamental consciousness. This is not just a shift in the depth of our own being, but in the depth of our relationship with everyone and everything that we encounter. We come into unmistakable contact with the luminous, unchanging essence that pervades all forms in nature. The essential unity of ourselves and others is present in every situation, and even painful encounters are infused with the love and clarity of our spiritual essence. From the subtle core of our being, all of our relationships become intimate and spiritual.

It is often taught that fundamental consciousness has no center and no circumference. It is a vast, boundless consciousness that pervades all of nature evenly. When we live in this subtle dimension of life, we experience that our own mind is a vast, open space, pervading everywhere. However, the teaching that fundamental consciousness has no center can be misleading. For in the human form there is an entranceway into fundamental consciousness that is, for each of us, its center. Connecting with this center, in the core of our being, is a direct and very effective way of realizing fundamental consciousness.

The entranceway into fundamental consciousness is the subtle channel that runs through the vertical core of the body from above the center of the crown of our head, to the center of the pubo-coccygeal muscle at the base of our torso. It has traditionally been described as a hair-thin straight line. When we contact it, we recognize it by its electric-like quality.

This channel is also our entranceway into our most subtle level of energy. We can view the human organism, and all other forms in nature, as having three dimensions: those of physical matter, energy and consciousness. These are really three levels of attunement to ourselves. The energy system itself is quite complex; it consists of many different types and subtleties of movement. The breath is part of the energy system. When we are primarily attuned to ourselves and the world as physical matter, as most people are, we experience our energy system only as our breath.

As we deepen our inward contact, we refine our attunement to ourselves. Then we realize that our breath moves everywhere in our body; it is part of a vast network of streaming movement and pulsation. We may also begin to see this subtle movement in the world around us, as light and vibration.

As we deepen our inward contact still further, we reach the subtle core of our body, and the dimension of fundamental consciousness. Now we experience that our energy not only moves through our whole body, but that it is unified with the energy that moves through our environment. At this point, we experience a more refined energy that moves through the subtle core of our body and branches out into our whole form. In the Hindu yoga system, this energy is called 'kundalini'. We experience our subtle core as an aliveness and fluidity in the innermost depth of our body. It feels as if something that has been rigid, unconscious and unknown has been transformed into something both conscious and flowing.

The subtle core of the body is the point of our deepest connection with our own being and our deepest perspective on life, our greatest distance from the people and objects around us. It is also our entranceway into oneness, our deepest and most subtle contact with everything around us. We arrive at our greatest distance from our environment and our oneness with our environment at the same time, by penetrating into the subtle core of the body.

When two people connect with each other from the subtle core of their bodies, they experience how fundamental consciousness pervades them both. They are each situated in the innermost depth of their own being, and one with each other at the same time. This feels like a connection across distance. At the same time it feels like the deepest connection we can have with another human being. There is an automatic resonance between the two cores, a kind of 'buzz'. This feels like the pure essence of contact, like contact itself. It is something like the contact that occurs when two people hum the same note, except that the resonance occurs spontaneously, we do not create it, and it occurs in the core of our body.

Along with this resonance, there is a spontaneous flow of very subtle energy that moves between the two cores. This energy is a type of communication that can lead to a deep, non-verbal understanding between partners. When two people relate with each other in the relational field of spiritual oneness, they experience that their relationship is made of both the unity and stillness of fundamental consciousness and the spontaneous exchange of subtle energy flow.

THE ESSENTIAL QUALITIES OF BEING

The subtle core of the body is the source of the essential qualities of our being. Fundamental consciousness is experienced as clear, luminous space – an unbroken emptiness that pervades all of our experience. Tibetan Buddhism describes this dimension as having the qualities of emptiness, clarity and bliss. Hindu metaphysics describes it as having the qualities of being, intelligence and bliss – *satchitananda* in Sanskrit. In the spiritual dimension, all of life is infused with emptiness or beingness, with luminosity and with bliss. The more realized we become, the more vividly we experience these three qualities pervading ourselves and our environment. Fundamental consciousness appears to have no other attributes aside from these three. It does not impose any other qualities of its own on our experience.

However, just as clear sunlight contains the simultaneous spectrum of all possible colors, our spiritual essence can also be said to contain, or to be composed of, all possible qualities of existence. This is because there is absolutely no difference between our essential being and our spiritual dimension. The one self of fundamental consciousness is the same self that we have always known ourselves to be, only clearly experienced.

The spectrum of all our essential qualities is clearly refracted in the subtle core of the human body. If we view the subtle core of the body from top to bottom, we can describe these qualities as awareness, emotion and physical sensation. The Hindu yoga system delineates this spectrum still further describing seven points along the core, called 'chakras', that are associated with subtle awareness, intuition, creativity, love, power, sexuality and gender.

The chakras are considered sensitive points where we can most easily penetrate into the subtle core. In traditional Hindu yoga, the first chakra at the base of the spine, the heart chakra and the brow chakra are also the location of knots (Sanskrit: *granthis*). In fact, we can unravel and release our complex knot of psychological defenses from the whole subtle core of the body. As we focus on these points, we develop the essential qualities of our being.

Although everyone experiences physical sensation, emotion and awareness, we reach the spiritual dimension of these qualities in the subtle core of our body. The spiritual dimension is a unity, an experience of all three qualities at once, pervading everywhere. It is an unchanging ground of awareness, emotion and physical sensation, within which specific, constantly changing awarenesses, emotions and sensations transpire.

The difference between what we might call ordinary awareness, emotion and physical sensation and the spiritual dimension of these qualities, is that in the spiritual dimension there is no separation between subject and object. For example, the same ground of awareness, emotion and physical sensation that experiences the table in my room also experiences myself sitting next to the table. Another way of saying this is, that both the table and my own form are pervaded by – or made of – the same unbroken ground of awareness, emotion and sensation. Yet a third way of saying this is, that the table and I both emerge simultaneously out of the same ground of awareness, emotion and sensation. The table and myself are experienced as a whole.

Although we attune to each of these three qualities through specific parts of the spectrum, they all pervade everywhere as fundamental consciousness. In other words, we attune to awareness through the upper third of the subtle core, but the quality of awareness pervades our whole being and environment at the same time. We attune to the quality of emotion through the mid-third of our subtle core, but the quality of emotion pervades everywhere. Likewise we attune to the quality of physical sensation through the bottom third of the subtle core and it pervades everywhere. Although this aspect of ourselves has not been spoken of much in the traditional religious teachings, the essence of physical sensation is an inseparable part of our individual wholeness and our spiritual oneness with all other life.

These essential qualities, entered through the subtle core of the body, make up the all-pervasive stillness of fundamental consciousness. When we reach the spiritual essence of these qualities, we become more open, more available for experience, and more deeply stimulated by life in all of these three aspects of ourselves.

Although fundamental consciousness is experienced as homogenous empty space, we can attune to this inherent spectrum of qualities in order to expand our realization of fundamental consciousness. This is important because, if we do not know about this spectrum of qualities, we tend to develop our spiritual realization only in that part of ourselves where we are most open, most in contact with ourselves, to begin with. So a mentally-oriented person will automatically meditate in his or her head. This will cultivate the quality of awareness while emotion and sensation remain constricted. This imbalanced development intensifies the psychological fragmentation that we each bring to our spiritual practice.

For example, Alex is a very intelligent friend of mine who has been meditating for over twenty years. He teaches philosophy in a university and is very articulate about his perceptions and ideas. There is, however, a distinct lack of engagement in the way he relates with people that makes him seem remote and disembodied. His meditation has focused solely on developing the centers in his forehead and crown chakras. It is not that he was taught to meditate only in his head, but he was not given any instruction about his body at all, so he naturally spends his meditation sessions inhabiting the same part of himself that he inhabits in his life. For Alex, there has been, since childhood, a fragmentation between the pain that he carries in his heart and the excitement of his mental faculties. Although I do not think he has formulated this consciously to himself, my impression is that he conceives of spiritual realization as a golden nothingness that will someday encompass him, and 'blot out' the emotional pain in his life once and for all. Yet he cannot become free of this pain without opening his heart.

Many traditional spiritual practices exacerbate this imbalance by instructing students to focus on only one area of their core, such as their heart center. Many popular spiritual teachings today focus solely on the mental practice of 'recognizing' nonduality. While this can be very helpful for stretching open the quality of awareness, it does not awaken the other aspects of fundamental consciousness. Over time, this imbalanced realization produces an uncomfortable predominance of experience in one area of our being.

The subtle core of the body is our entranceway into fundamental consciousness, and at the same time, it is the source of the essential qualities of our being. The capacity of our being for awareness, emotion and sensation does not vanish as we realize ourselves as fundamental consciousness – it deepens and matures into its essence. It becomes free of psychological constrictions; free and available for the changing content of experience. Spiritual realization and personal development are therefore one and the same process. Even a yogi sitting alone in his or her cave comes into the fullness of being that develops with the realization of fundamental consciousness.

This process also develops our ability to be intimate. Awareness, emotion and physical sensation are not just the qualities of our individual being, they are also the qualities of oneness, and the three major pathways of our exchange with other people. When we connect from the core of our own body to the core of someone else's body, we are in a spiritual relationship with them. We are able to relate to them from the most authentic and pristine source of our love, understanding and sensation.

PENETRATING INTO THE SUBTLE CORE

It is difficult to make an exact correspondence between our physical anatomy and the subtle core of the body. The core is sometimes described as the innermost core of our spinal cord. But the subtle core of the body is a straight line from top to bottom, while the spine is not. It has also been said that the subtle core of the body is in front of the spine. Again, we cannot prove or disprove this. It is, however, most effective to focus inward towards the spine from the front of one's body.

We can best locate the subtle core of the body by the way it feels. There is an unmistakable electrical quality in the core that is our most trustworthy guide. There is also a sense of essence, or truth, in the core of the body that is difficult to convey in words, but which is easy to recognize when you come to it. In order to attune to this most subtle aspect of ourselves, it is necessary to make our focus extremely subtle and precise. This refined focus can penetrate into the subtle core.

In Subtle Self Work, we usually practice accessing the subtle core from three main points: the center of the head, the center of the chest, and the center of the pelvis.

The center of the head is located within the internal space of the head, between the ears. When we attune to the center of the head, we develop the awareness aspect of the fundamental consciousness that pervades all of our experience, both internal and external.

The heart center is exactly the same as the Hindu heart chakra, and it is located in the center of the chest, deep in the subtle core of the body. Through this center, we develop the emotion aspect of fundamental consciousness. The more we open the knot of the heart center, the more the emotional ground of our being feels like pure love, or bliss. This blissful feeling pervades all of our experience, even that of a painful emotion like grief or anger.

The pelvic center is two or three finger widths below the navel, in the subtle core of the body. It is between the second and third chakras in the Hindu system, and it is through this center that we develop the physical sensation aspect of fundamental consciousness.

At the end of this chapter there is an exercise for accessing one's own core and connecting with another person from each of these points. For everyone, there will be parts of the core that are more difficult to access than others. We each have our own pattern of psychological defense that blocks our inward contact with ourselves in particular parts of our body. We have to penetrate through these rigidities in order to contact the core, and this is a process which often brings childhood feelings and memories to the surface. For example, people sometimes experience a release of grief as they contact their heart chakra. However, the more access we have to our core, the easier it becomes to recognize and release these holding patterns.

THE INTEGRATIVE AXIS

The subtle core of the body is the integrative axis of our being and when we contact the core within our pelvis, chest and head, we integrate the essential qualities of our being. This means that we can sense, feel and understand at the same time. This integration is also the maturity, or the most subtle range, of all three essential qualities. When we can think, feel and sense with our whole being, we become capable of blissful emotion and sensation, and original, intuitive thinking.

When two people relate to each other from all three points within the core of their bodies, it can help expand the range of their exchange with each other. When a couple is having difficulty communicating, it is often because each one is more open in, or more in contact with, different qualities of their being. For example, one person may live mostly in their awareness, while the other lives mostly in their emotional capacity. This will influence both the manner and the content of each person's communication with the other. And it will effect something more subtle, as I described above. There will be a lack of 'resonance' between them that will make them feel mysteriously out of sync with each other. This imbalance can be resolved by connecting with each other 'core-to-core' from the pelvis, chest and head.

Last year, for example, a couple named Margaret and Carl came to see me. They had known each other only a few months and were on the point of splitting up. Although they enjoyed their sexual relationship very much, and also felt an unusually strong emotional connection, they still had great difficulty communicating. They found conversation with each other difficult and even boring, and had concluded that they were not really suited for each other. However, because of the depth of their sexual and emotional connection they were unable to face the pain of losing each other. They both felt bewildered and trapped by the intensity of their bond.

During the first session I taught them the exercise of contacting the subtle core of their own bodies within the three points of pelvis, chest and head. They were both able to do this immediately. I then gave them the exercise of connecting with each other from the subtle core of their bodies. They could connect with each other easily from the pelvis and chest points. When they connected from the subtle core of their chests (their heart chakras), there was an immediate and powerful resonance, and a flow of love between them that both delighted and embarrassed them. They were, however, unable to feel the resonance of connection in their head centers, which I thought was interesting, because they had both been able to contact their head centers easily alone.

When I pointed this out to them, Margaret was able to explain the difficulty. She acknowledged to me, in a tone that suggested I would know exactly what she meant, that men did not appreciate a woman who was too mentally alert. As she was still in the 'courtship' phase of her relationship with Carl, and in fact had never been beyond that phase with any man, she said that she was making herself as attractive as possible by 'dimming' her awareness.

Carl seemed genuinely shocked that Margaret would think he required her to be less intelligent than she was. We both encouraged her to take the chance of bringing all of herself to the relationship. We repeated the exercise and this time they attuned at once to each other's quality of awareness. Then Carl began to cry. He had never before felt this mental intimacy with a woman. He said he felt 'connected all the way through' with another human being.

This exercise is a very effective way to recognize the subjective organization that each person brings to the relational field, because couples can experience for themselves where the exchange between them is blocked. The exercise also helps penetrate through the defenses that are obstructing their contact. As they continue to practice it, they will be able to unravel the complex skein of bound feelings, memories and beliefs that produce the difficulties in their relationship.

THE HINDU CHAKRA SYSTEM

As I said, the Hindu chakra system divides the continuum of physical sensation, emotion and awareness into seven main points along the core. These are located at the base of the spine, in the sacral area, the navel area, the center of the chest, the base of the throat, the center of the head (or between the brows) and at the center of the top of the head. It is very helpful to focus on these points in order to expand one's realization of fundamental consciousness. Couples can also practice attuning to each other from each of these points. The chakra system is particularly useful for addressing specific problems in relationships.

About a year ago, a couple, named Laura and Jack, came to work with me as a last resort before ending their relationship. They had been together for five years and cared deeply for each other. They also shared a lively intellectual connection, and it was this that they most dreaded having to give up if their relationship ended. But neither was satisfied with their sexual intimacy. Jack felt that their sexual difficulties did not matter that much, but Laura said she missed having passion in her life and could not continue with Jack unless their sexual relationship improved.

When I taught them the exercise of attuning to each other from the three points along the core, they were able to experience the resonance between them in the center of the head and heart, but not in the pelvic center. Jack was unable to bring his focus deeply enough inside his pelvis to reach the subtle core of his body. I then asked them to direct their focus into the second chakra, in the area of the sacrum. This point is a little lower than the pelvic center, and it is associated specifically with sexuality.

As they attempted to contact each other from their second chakras, Jack said he felt that he was tightening up even more. By observing himself closely as he tightened against sexual contact with Laura, he realized that this movement of shutting down his sexual sensation was very familiar. As he continued to practice this exercise over the next few sessions, Jack remembered the injunctions against sexual feelings that he had learned in his family home. He had never been aware of his parents having any sexual feelings for each other, had never even seen them embrace. Gradually, he had tightened his own pelvis against his early stirrings of sexual feelings until it matched the tightness in his parent's bodies. As he brought his focus more deeply within his pelvis, he remembered several incidents in his childhood in which he had felt ashamed of his genitals. The worst was the time his mother had suddenly burst into his room as he was masturbating and threatened to tell their priest. With these insights, Jack was able to gradually release the tightness in his pelvis, and attune to the subtle core of his pelvis.

However, as Jack gained contact with his sexuality, Laura began to shut down. She found that she was afraid to feel contact with Jack from the core of her pelvis. We then entered another phase of work in which Laura remembered the frightening situations she had encountered when she reached puberty. There were groups of men in her neighborhood who would sit outside the old brownstone buildings and make aggressive sexual remarks to the young girls who walked by. They made particular jokes about her breasts and would sometimes walk after her, making loud kissing sounds. At home she had to fend off the sexual innuendoes and advances of her uncles. One of these men had finally forced her to have sex with him when Laura was still a virgin. All of her adult life, she had carefully chosen men who did not make any demands on her sexually. Gradually, with Jack's gentle support, Laura was able to overcome her fear and allow herself to feel sexual contact from her core to his. With practice, they added the sexual dimension to the love and intellectual contact which they already shared.

Another chakra that is often important for couples is the third chakra, associated with power. This point is located on the level of the navel, in the core of the body. Many people have difficulty experiencing the essential quality of power. For women this is usually because they have been taught that any display of power is unfeminine, whereas men often shut down their power early in life so as not to resemble male family members or cultural stereotypes whose power seemed brutal or dominating. So both men and women may grow up feeling powerless. When we feel powerless, we often attempt to protect ourselves from being overpowered by another person, by weakening them in whatever way we can. This leads to the power struggles that challenge so many relationships. The most effective resolution for power struggles is for both people involved to gain a true sense of their own power. By focusing within the third chakra they can each develop power as an experienced quality in their body. When they connect with each other from their third chakras, they can experience the equality of true contact, rather than a struggle for dominance.

Although they do not appear on most charts of the chakras, there are several points above the head that can also be contacted. For couples interested in spiritual realization, it can be helpful to connect with each other from the eighth chakra, a few inches above the center of the top of the head. Again, this point can be located best by its electrical quality. If you cannot actually feel this point, you can begin by imagining a candle flame above your head. Just by keeping your focus on the space above your head, you will eventually become sensitive to the actual quality of the chakra. Any exercise of focusing on the space above one's head should be followed by 'grounding' exercises such as inhabiting the feet, legs and pelvis, and focusing within the pelvic center in the core of the pelvis.

It is important to understand that the practice of accessing one's core and connecting core-to-core with one's partner is just an exercise. We should be careful not to hold on to any position in ourselves. However, as we continue to practice attuning to the subtle core of our body, we will find ourselves experiencing life from the perspective and integration of our core, without any effort. Couples will find that they gradually gain more continuity with each other. In other words, they both become more open to the dimension of spiritual oneness. This frees the flow of energy between them, and all of their communication becomes more authentic and spontaneous.

People often ask whether it is possible to relate core-to-core with people who are not attuned to the subtle core of their own bodies. Once we begin to live in the subtle core of our body as an ongoing experience, we do relate to everyone and everything we encounter from the core of our body. When we relate to someone who is not attuned to the core of their own body, we will not experience the same depth of contact that we feel with someone who is in the subtle core. This can be a valuable guide if we are searching for an intimate partner, because we can experience whether a person is meeting us at the same depth that we know ourselves, and whether the points of contact are sexual, emotional or mental. This can also help us understand our relationships with other important people in our lives, such as relatives and co-workers.

If we have felt that someone, for example a parent or a spouse, has not loved or understood us, it can be healing for our own psychological wounds to experience that person clearly from the subtle core of our body. Many sensitive people have grown up feeling unlovable and unrecognizable because the depth of their own feelings and awareness was not met by their family. They often describe a sense of being on the 'wrong planet', of wishing that they could 'call home' the way ET did in the movie. By relating with family members from the subtle core of our body, we may see that they simply did not have the inward contact with themselves that would have made them capable of the love and awareness we needed. This makes it easier to forgive both ourselves and them for the problems in the relationship. It enables us to stop waiting for them to finally recognize and love us, and to disentangle ourselves from the confines of that old relationship. This healing can even occur by imagining the person in front of us, and relating to their image from the subtle core of our head, chest and pelvis.

People often express the fear that they will be completely isolated if they live in the deeper perspective of their spiritual core. From my own experience, and my observation of other people's lives, I have come to trust that, if we are open to relationship, we will always find people with whom we can be truly intimate, whatever depth we grow to in ourselves. I have also found that living in the subtle core of the body helps us feel more kinship with people in general. We can see clearly the defenses that keep people from truly loving each other, and recognize that they are similar to the defenses that we have encountered in ourselves. The subtle core of our body is our entranceway into the oneness of fundamental consciousness. Although there may be only a few individuals with whom we can enjoy 'core-to-core' contact, we gain an ongoing sense of intimacy with life as a whole.

DISENTANGLING FROM THE CORE

There are many ways to practice attuning to the points within the core of the body that can facilitate spiritual realization. For example, it is helpful, when you contact each of these points, to feel that you are in the very center of the all-pervasive space of fundamental consciousness. You can experience that the subtle core of the body opens out into fundamental consciousness, in all directions.

One of the most effective ways of working with the subtle core of the body is to absorb one's attention into it. In Tibetan Buddhism they speak of absorbing the 'subtle winds' into the core. The meaning of this instruction will become clear as you absorb your attention into the core. You will feel that you are living and breathing within the whole core. This absorption helps fill in the fragmentation in our contact with the core, and stabilizes our realization of fundamental consciousness.

You can also practice letting go of yourself from – or as – the subtle core. As the subtle core of the body, we experience life without gripping or grasping at it. We allow life to be exactly as it is, to flow. As we unravel the knot of our being from the subtle core of the body, we can actually feel that we are disentangling from all of the content of our experience. We are becoming free. There is a sense that who we really are is, literally, letting go of whatever we are not.

As I explained in chapter one, the disentanglement of fundamental consciousness from the content of experience can help us feel less possessive in our relationships. As an exercise, the subtle core of the body can be used specifically for letting go of our entanglements with other people. For example, we can contact a point within our core, while picturing a parent or some other important person from our life. As we initiate our breath from this point (following the instructions in exercise 4), we can allow ourselves to let go of our grip on the image of that person. Although this is an imaginal exercise, we may find that our grip on the image is actual; that it involves an actual holding pattern in our breath and body. It is this holding pattern that will dissolve as we disentangle ourselves from the image.

Not long ago, a woman named Gwendolyn came to work with me because she was suffering such severe depression that she was spending most of her time in bed. She was in her mid-seventies, and had a successful career as a freelance book editor, but that was falling apart as she increasingly turned down work. She told me that her husband had died three years before. Although her friends all felt that it was time to end her mourning and 'get on with her life', she did not feel capable of going on without him. They had been married for fifty-two years. As we spoke about her long marriage, I was struck by her lack of emotion. It turned out that, although she had withdrawn from her life, she had not yet begun to mourn. She had barely cried since his death. She felt that, if she allowed herself to grieve, she might get over the loss of him; she might finally lose him.

I taught Gwendolyn the exercise of picturing her husband in front of her as she contacted each of the three points within the core of her body. I asked her to picture him as she inhaled and exhaled from within these points. At first she found that as she inhaled she pulled his image closer to her, and she worked with this for a while, pulling him in and pushing him away with her breath. Then I asked her to make her breath more subtle, so that it felt like she was breathing a mixture of breath and consciousness.

Gwendolyn was amazed at how subtle she had to make her breath in order not to effect the image in front of her. Just as our entanglement with life is so subtle that most people never notice it, the process of disentanglement requires a very refined, precise inward attunement. With practice, she was able to feel less attached to the image of her husband. Although she could picture him vividly, she no longer felt that her own being was bound up with his. She was finally able to feel the pain of separation from him, and to allow her tears to flow. Gradually, her grief subsided and she regained her vitality.

EXERCISE 4
RELATING CORE TO CORE

Partners sit facing each other on chairs, or cross-legged on cushions on the floor, with backs straight.

Close your eyes. Mentally locate a point in the center of your own head, between your ears. There will be an electric-like quality to this point when you find it. Some people have described it as coming into a point of light within the relative darkness of the head. It is important to experience this point, not to visualize it. Also, make sure that you are not too high in your head. You should be able to feel the bottom of your torso just by being in the center of your head as there is an automatic resonance down through the whole subtle core when you are in the center of your head.

Inhale by bringing the breath through your nostrils and into the center of your head. The breath comes in through both nostrils and then becomes a single stream of breath that can penetrate through your head to the center. Exhale through your nostrils.

Now initiate the breath from the center of your head. The center of your head draws in the breath on the inhale, and releases the breath on the exhale. The breath will still enter and exit through your nostrils, but it will feel like the center of your head is inhaling and exhaling. It should feel as if the center of the head inhales a mixture of breath and consciousness, or as if the mind is breathing inside the center of your head.

Open your eyes and remain in the center of your head. Make eye contact with your partner, across the distance between you. Be aware of how much distance there is between you as you look at your partner. It will probably feel as if you become further away from your partner.

Find the center of your head again. From the center of your own head, *mentally find the center of your partner's head. Be careful that you do not leave the center of your own head as you do this. You do not have to move at all to find the center of your partner's head. When you are able to do this you will feel a resonance between the center of your head and your partner's head.*

Close your eyes, and again mentally find the center of your own head. From the center of your head, find a point in the center of your chest, as deeply inward as you can bring your focus. You will recognize it by its electric-like quality. This is your heart center.

Now initiate your inhale from inside your heart center. It feels as if the heart center itself draws in the breath. Your exhale is a release from inside your heart center. As you practice this, let your breath become increasingly subtle and silent, until it feels as if the heart center draws in a mixture of breath and consciousness, or as if the mind is breathing inside the heart center.

Open your eyes and, staying in your heart center, make eye contact with your partner. Again, be aware of the distance between the two of you as you make eye contact.

From your heart center, find the heart center of your partner. Be careful that you do not leave your heart center as you find the heart center of your partner. Try to trust that you will be able to connect with your partner from your core, without coming out of yourself. There is a particular tendency, in the heart center, to project our love towards other people, so as to convince them that we really do love them. However, the projection of love is really less heartfelt than the core-to-core connection, because it separates us from the source of our love in our core.

Close your eyes and, again, mentally find the center of your own head. From the center of your head, find a point about two or three finger widths below your navel, but as deeply inward as you can bring your focus. You will recognize it by its electric-like quality. This is your pelvic center.

Initiate your inhale from inside your pelvic center. It feels as if the pelvic center itself draws in the breath. Your exhale is a release from inside your pelvic center. Again, the breath will feel like a mixture of breath and consciousness, or as if the mind is breathing inside the pelvic center.

Open your eyes, and staying in your pelvic center, make eye contact with your partner. Be aware of the distance between you both as you make eye contact. Now, from your pelvic center, find the pelvic center of your partner. Be careful that you do not leave your pelvic center as you find the pelvic center of your partner.

Close your eyes, and find the center of your own head. Now find the center of your head and your heart center at the same time. And find all three centers at the same time: the center of your head, your heart center and your pelvic center.

Initiate your breath from all three centers at the same time. Your exhale is a release from within all three centers. Be patient with yourself; this will probably take a little practice. Feel that all three centers breathe in a mixture of breath and consciousness, or that the mind is breathing in all three centers.

Stay in all three centers as you open your eyes and make eye contact with your partner. Be aware of the distance between you. Staying in all three centers in your own core, find all three centers in your partner's core. Stay in your own core as you do this.

CHAPTER FOUR

Mutual Contact

All fully awakened beings abide inseparably in the expanse of
Primordial Awareness, and all are in essence one.[9]

Once we have awakened to the spiritual dimension of
ourselves, we live in an ongoing experience of unity, or
inseparability, with everything that we encounter. We live in a
dimension of internal spaciousness, and stillness, that renders
all experience fundamentally equal – 'one taste'. It is also a
dimension of luminosity and sweetness or, as we become
more open, blissfulness. The unity, brightness and bliss of
spiritual consciousness infuses all of our relationships: with
people, with nature, and even with inanimate things.

However, our relationships differ according to the various
things and beings we encounter. One important difference is
the degree of mutual contact that can be experienced in each
of these relationships. For example, someone who has realized
fundamental consciousness can make great contact with a
table. First of all, they feel unified with the table: the clear-
through empty space of spiritual consciousness pervades both
the table and themselves. When they put their hand on the
table, they can touch it all the way through its depth, so that
they feel not only the texture of the table's surface, but also
the vibratory quality of the wood. They may even feel a flow
of love from their own heart towards the table, if the table has
been in their life for many years, for example. But the table
itself makes no discernible response, either to their touch or

---

9 Jig-me Ling-pa, *The Dzog-chen Innermost Essence Preliminary Practice*, trans. Ven. Tulku
   Thondup (Dharamasala, India: Library of Tibetan Works & Archives, 1982), p.64

their love. It is a safe bet that the table is not even aware of this person in any way, and certainly has no sense of blissful unity with them.

If the same person puts their hand on a living tree, however, they will feel some small response to their touch. Although I am sure some would argue this point, many people who have spent time communing with nature will agree that the communing is not strictly a one-way affair; there is a small degree of mutuality to the contact. But if this person puts their hand on an animal – a cat, for example – he will feel even more response to their touch. I am not speaking about a response like purring or scratching, but rather a mutuality of the touch itself. We could describe this as a 'touching back' from the cat to the person, but it is not a volitional activity, rather it is an automatic, spontaneous result of the meeting of two conscious beings. Also, this mutual touch between person and cat is not just a tactile experience: it involves the person's whole being and the cat's whole being. It is made of the essential qualities of being: awareness, emotion and physical sensation.

There is more mutual contact with a cat than with a tree because a cat is more conscious than a tree. Contact is a function of consciousness. A cat is more conscious of its environment than a tree, and probably more conscious of its internal experience as well. In the terms that I have been using in this book, the cat is more open than the tree to the relational field of self and other.

For this same reason, there is more potential for mutual contact with a human being than with a cat. Human beings are complex, so we can have different kinds of contact with different human beings, depending upon each of our organizations of openness and defense in the aspects of awareness, emotion and physical sensation. This organization is not entirely static; it shifts with the development of trust, and other factors. But again, I am not speaking here of action or behavior. Mutual contact is an experience of spontaneous resonance that can occur with anyone who is open to life in the same ways that we are.

The greatest degree of mutual contact occurs between two people who have both realized fundamental consciousness. When we connect with another person in the oneness of the spiritual dimension, we recognize them by the depth and intensity of our mutual contact. Zen Buddhism says of this encounter, 'Like two thieves in the night, they recognize each other at once.'

When two people meet in the dimension of fundamental consciousness, they experience themselves as a continuity of awareness, love or bliss, and physical sensation. As I described in the last chapter, the spiritual dimension of these three qualities is quite different from conventional experience. It does not just feel, for example, that one is aware of the other, or that one loves or senses the other, but that they are made of a single presence of awareness, love and physical sensation. Contact is an inherent component of the continuity of presence. Within this unified presence there is also a meeting of the two people's energy systems, which flow spontaneously between them. This energy carries their exchange of specific mental, emotional and tactile communications.

Interestingly, contact does not require spatial proximity. As we become more open to life, we find that we have the ability to contact people at a distance. The first time I experienced this was in my early twenties. I had enrolled in a Silva Mind Control course to help me overcome my addiction to cigarettes. I don't remember the teacher's name but I can still picture her vibrant face. On the last day of the three-day course, I overslept. I was awakened by a strange, unembodied 'nudge' that I recognized at once as the presence of the teacher. This sort of contact is volitional, but it is a function of the subtle consciousness that pervades and unifies all life.

THE QUALITIES OF CONTACT

We can divide, or categorize, the unity of our essential being in many different ways. For example, the Tibetan Buddhists describe the spiritual dimension as having, or being made of, three qualities: emptiness, luminosity and bliss (Tibetan: *tongpa*, *salwa*, *dewa*). The Hindus say that it has the qualities of being, intelligence and bliss (Sanskrit: *sat*, *chit*, *ananda*). In Subtle Self Work I divide it into essential awareness, emotion and physical sensation. We can also divide the human organism into consciousness, energy and matter, or into the motionless ground of experience and the changing content of experience. These are all schematic divisions of something that is essentially indivisible.

This chapter looks at the essential qualities of awareness, emotion and physical sensation. Within the unchanging stillness of these essential qualities, we experience the movement of specific perceptions, cognitions, emotions and sensations. (I will be looking at the subject of perception separately in chapter five).

Awareness, emotion and physical sensation are three modalities of experience, three arenas of openness to the spontaneous flow of life. They are also three aspects of our contact with other people. As we deepen all three qualities in ourselves, our responses to life, and our contact with other people gain richness, complexity, and range.

One of the major principles of wholeness is that all of the 'parts' contain all of the other parts. For example, the essential nature of our little finger is awareness, emotion, and physical sensation. We have the ability to attune to each of these qualities separately, or to experience them as a unity. The purpose of attuning to each of the essential qualities separately is in order to recognize and release the defenses that specifically constrict each of them. As this release occurs, the fragmentations between these aspects of our being dissolve. As the fragmentations within our own being dissolve, the fragmentations between ourselves and other people also dissolve.

In the spiritual dimension of ourselves, we are free. This is not a freedom from life; it is a freedom of life. It means that our being itself is free; that our awareness, love and sensation are available to receive and respond to life. The more we attune to fundamental consciousness, the more our thoughts, feelings, sensations, perceptions and actions seem to emerge directly from the empty, all-pervasive space of fundamental consciousness.

Just as our essential qualities are actually an indivisible continuum, the body, in its undefended state, provides an integrated unity of these three types of experience. There is, at root, no difference – no separation – between the physical body and the most subtle dimension of consciousness. The essential nature of the physical body is fundamental consciousness. We cannot hold the physical body tight and loosen consciousness at the same time.

There is a direct correlation between the areas where we are open or defended in our body, and our degree of attunement to the qualities of awareness, emotion and physical sensation. However all of the qualities of our being pervade our whole body. For example, even though we need to be open in the upper third of our body and to be able to access the upper third of the subtle core of our body, in order to reach the essential quality of awareness, this quality pervades our whole body. This means that, as we realize the spiritual dimension of ourselves, we are able to experience awareness, emotion and physical sensation with our whole being.

This is easier to experience than to grasp intellectually (See the exercise at the end of this chapter.) However, I think it can best be understood in the light of the self-similarity theory of fractals. Although this subject is beyond the scope of this book, I will say briefly that, according to self-similarity theory, each form in nature is made of one pattern repeated throughout itself on different scales. A branch of a tree, for example, mirrors the form of the tree itself. In this same way, the spectrum of awareness/emotion/physical sensation that makes up the whole body, is also repeated in each of the body's parts, no matter how small.

We can see the application of this principle in bodywork techniques such as foot reflexology, in which different parts of the body can be energized by stimulating corresponding parts of the foot. The correspondence is very simple: it is as if the general shape of the body were imprinted on the foot. For example rubbing the toes energizes the top of the body, and rubbing the heel energizes the base of the body. In fact, any part of the body can be used in the same way. In *Jin Shin Jyutsu*, rubbing the tips of the toes stimulates the top of the body, and rubbing the base of the toes stimulates the bottom of the body. Hand reflexology uses the correspondence of the hand to the whole body for healing.

Thus a defensive constriction in the head limits our awareness, and it also produces a constriction throughout our whole being. Likewise, to release a constriction in our head will deepen our capacity for awareness and will also produce more openness throughout our whole being.

Along with specific holding patterns in each of these three aspects of experience, we also create artificial fragmentations between them. We separate our awareness from our emotions, our emotions from our physical – and sexual – sensations, and so on. As we reach the spiritual dimension of ourselves, we are able to perceive, think, feel and sense at the same time. Each moment of our lives registers as a unity of perception, cognition, emotion and sensation, which enriches all of our interactions with other people. For example, our physical contact with other people is integrated with emotion and awareness, which enables us to have a more intimate relationship with another person.

AWARENESS

The essential quality of awareness is a wide-open mental clarity that pervades our whole body and our environment at the same time. In religious terms, it is gnosis, an ongoing experience of knowing God. In relationships with other people, it is an ongoing mental connectedness.

As we open to this aspect of fundamental consciousness, we gain the spontaneity of our mental faculties. We are available for the inspiration of our own unique thoughts. Original, spontaneous thought is the natural, essential function of the human mind. Although civilization always tends towards conformity, we can gradually free ourselves from the hypnotic influence that our family and culture have had on our minds.

To live in the essential quality of awareness also means to be receptive to the intellectual stimuli around us. Many sensitive people shut out the ideas and opinions of other people because they know how easily they lose track of their own inner voice. I knew one man who did not even read books, because he feared the intrusion of other people's knowledge, but this defensive tactic had left him mulling over ideas that came to him many years ago in his youth, which were by now too familiar to excite him. Our awareness is an important aspect of the 'open system' in which we grow. Awareness is also a vital part of our intimacy with other people. It can be as pleasurable to be mentally aroused by another person as it is to be moved emotionally and physically.

When we live in our essential awareness, we have our own unique understanding of life, our own perspective. This understanding is not static; it keeps developing, but it retains its unique identity, as characteristic of our individual being as the sound of our voice. It is formed by our specific design of openness and defense, which is our individual perspective on wholeness, and by our unique path of unwinding towards wholeness.

We have all heard stories of saints and prophets receiving 'revelations' from the spiritual dimension. The process of spiritual development is revelatory for everyone, however. It is important to remain open to the unfolding of our own insight; not to drown it out with the static revelation of religious teachings or the generalized messages of commercially driven media. This is important for us collectively as well as personally. When we can hear and express our spontaneous thoughts, we help to bring truth into the world. Even if we do not relate with many people, we help our culture become more intelligent and authentic, we help it progress in its understanding of reality.

It is sometimes taught that spiritual realization means having no thoughts. Many initial meditation techniques are designed for emptying the mind. For example, there is a technique in Zen Buddhism in which the meditator attempts to count ten consecutive breaths, returning to the number one each time she has a thought. This technique can help us gradually eliminate the surface 'mental chatter' or habitual 'tape loops' that prevent us from settling into more subtle levels of consciousness. But the more advanced Buddhist teachings speak of a 'non-abiding' mind in which the movement of our thoughts flows through the stillness and emptiness of our being without disturbing, or altering it in any way. In *Zen Mind, Beginner's Mind*, Zen Master Shunryu Suzuki writes, 'To stop your mind does not mean to stop the activities of mind. It means your mind pervades your whole body.'[10] As we reach the all-pervasive dimension of consciousness, we realize that our awareness is an all-pervasive stillness. But within this stillness, our thoughts move freely and spontaneously.

Spiritual realization is also described as a lack of 'mental elaboration' on our experience. This means that we do not project our past experience onto the present. We do not obscure our awareness of the present moment with preconceptions and fantasies. We live in what Zen calls 'don't know mind'. Some students of Buddhism interpret this phrase to mean a complete lack of cognition, suggesting that spiritual realization means living in a world of perceptual stimuli without any cognitive recognition of these stimuli. But I believe this is a mistaken reading of the teaching. 'Don't know mind' is a cognition that is fresh in each moment, that is not limited either by repression or projection. It means that we allow each moment to arrive unanticipated and unmodified. A Tibetan Buddhist text describes the spiritual dimension as the 'total field of events and *meanings*'[11] (italics mine). Another text calls it 'the great empty cognizance'[12]. It is the nature of essential awareness to know.

---

10 Shunryu Suzuki, *Zen Mind, Beginner's Mind* (New York: Weatherhill, 1980), p.41

11 Manjusrimitra, *Primordial Experience*, trans. Namkhai Norbu, Kennard Lipman (Boston: Shambhala, 1987), p.xiii

12 Tsele Natsok Rangdrol, *The Circle of the Sun*, trans. Erik Pema Kunsang (Hong Kong: Rangjung Yeshe Publications, 1990), p.72

The essential quality of awareness is our ordinary awareness, clearly experienced. It is the most relaxed, natural condition of our awareness. In order to relax our awareness we need to relax those parts of our physical body that are associated with mental activity. Most people have defensive holding patterns and habitual ways of being that produce constriction in their heads. One of the most common reasons that we constrict our awareness as children is to accommodate our parents' view of reality, or the view of reality that our parents want us to have. For example, there may be a tacit family agreement not to notice the drunken behavior of one of the family members. Or our parents may fear that we will outwit them, or in some way gain the upper hand, if we are allowed to have our own opinions. We may be told, either outright or through more subtle messages that we are 'too smart for our own good', or something of this sort.

Because of these defensive patterns, and because of the ways we have mirrored the openness and defense of our parents, and because of other more mysterious factors such as talent, we all use some aspects of our mental faculties more than others. This means that most of us inhabit, and use, some parts of our brain more than other parts. As we realize fundamental consciousness, we are able to inhabit our whole brain at once. Then our mental processes include the whole range of our mental abilities, including intuition and imagination. This greatly enhances both our understanding and our creativity.

Relaxing into the essential quality of awareness produces a profound change in the way we relate with the world. I worked with a woman who grew up in an atmosphere of intense intellectual competition. Her father seemed capable of relating only on an intellectual level with his children, and his rare gestures of approval were always awarded for displays of mental ability. She remembered dinner time as a battlefield of aggressively dazzling conversation. If she was not able to match or better her brother's demonstration of verbal prowess and of knowledge, she would become the target of her father's disdainful humor. This was so painful for her that she would always come to the dinner table with a prepared presentation of some topic that she had selected from a magazine or newspaper. As an adult, she still felt it necessary to stand out intellectually in any social situation. Even for parties, she would prepare a topic of conversation that she could discuss articulately and in depth.

When I met her she described a feeling of tightness, like a fist in her brain, that never went away. She also complained of feeling unreal, as if she were always pretending to be smarter than she really was. As she practiced attuning to the awareness aspect of fundamental consciousness, the tightness in her brain relaxed and, after several months, she reported feeling that her mind was both 'inside and all around her' but it was 'resting'. She could feel her intelligence as an ongoing presence so that, for the first time in her life, she knew without doubt that she was not stupid. She described this constant presence as a 'brightness and clarity without effort'. She practiced going 'as is' to parties, without a prepared speech. She found that she could sit there silently – in the beginning with studied concentration, and then finally with ease – until something actually occurred to her to say. The spontaneity of her thoughts delighted her. 'Sometimes I don't even say them out loud', she told me, 'I just enjoy them myself.' Without the pressure to perform competitively, she could take pleasure in her intelligence, as well as in the thoughts and ideas of the people around her.

The quality of awareness is often used as a path to spiritual realization. Some teachers say that we can achieve spiritual unity by being attentive to each moment. If we sit still and simply attend to each present moment, we will, very gradually, let go of our holding patterns and deepen towards the spiritual dimension. However, the most deeply engrained defensive patterns will probably not succumb to this tech-nique, or at least not for a very long while. It is also important to understand that all attention is not equal. Because of our deeply held defensive patterns, we may remain in a more superficial awareness of the present moment and not reach the very subtle awareness that is the spiritual dimension.

Some other methods of realizing essential awareness are the attunement to the subtle core of the head, as I described in the last chapter, or attunement directly to the quality of awareness, as in the exercise at the end of this chapter. Some Zen koans also work on releasing the 'awareness knot' by directing the full force of one's mental faculties on an unanswerable, mind-blowing riddle. All of these approaches are 'stretches' for the quality of awareness. They can help deliver us, in increments, towards spiritual freedom.

It is important, however, to recognize that awareness is not the whole nature of spiritual oneness. Since our organism is a unity, we might conclude that stretching open the quality of awareness will open our whole being, and this is true to some extent. But our qualities of emotion and physical sensation are often so deeply, and unconsciously, constricted that opening only the quality of awareness actually intensifies our fragmentation. Also, because the rigid holding patterns in our body make it uncomfortable for us to inhabit our body, there is a common tendency for people to place their awareness in the world around them and feel that they have achieved the 'nonexistence' of the separate self. But the spiritual 'emptiness' of the self – the unity of self and environment – is always based on internal contact with our own individual form. Wherever we are in contact with the internal space of our body – wherever we inhabit our body – we become open to life. It is this openness of our own form that allows us to live in the unity of self and other.

EMOTION

The essential quality of emotion is distinguishable from the qualities of awareness and physical sensation. As we become more attuned to this aspect of fundamental consciousness, we begin to experience it as sweetness, or love. We experience an ongoing, unwavering subtle quality of love pervading our body and our environment at the same time. This is unconditional and unconditioned love. It is not love for someone or something; it is love itself.

This unwavering love is not disturbed by the movement of our specific emotional responses. We can experience a wave of sadness or a surge of fury moving through the ongoing quality of love in our body, without disturbing it. In fact, our specific emotions become deeper and more spontaneous as we realize the essential quality of emotion. But they also become more appropriate to our actual circumstances; less triggered, and less intensified, by our projections of past events onto the present. Arising directly out of the essence of our being, our emotions are entirely fluid and transient. Whether or not we express them, they flow through us and dissipate without a trace.

No one reaches adulthood without some degree of emotional constriction. We defend ourselves against feeling emotional pain by arresting the energetic flow of our emotions. If this is repeated over time – or if the arrested emotional response is particularly intense – the muscular action required to bind the response becomes a chronic pattern of tension in our body. The whole moment of response is caught in this arrested flow, so that our holding patterns contain both the memory of the painful event and the unspent energy of the emotional charge. In this way, we actually hold old grief, anger and fear within our organism. These bound emotions color our present experience. For example, no matter how much we know of our childhood history, the grief held within our body will continue to make life seem sad to us as adults, until that arrested grief is allowed to flow and discharge.

Most people need to have released some degree of their bound emotional pain before they are able to realize fundamental consciousness. However, once we have realized the spiritual dimension, we can accelerate the process of emotional release. As fundamental consciousness, we are, in a sense, deeper than our emotional binding. The spiritual dimension does not hold onto anything. It is, by definition, disentangled from all of the content of experience.

For a year I worked with a man with a long history of depression, and almost as long a history of psychotherapy. When I first met Paul, I thought of the phrase 'sad sack' because he was so huddled into himself and deflated. He cried continuously as he told me about his sad childhood, how he was abandoned by both parents by the age of four, sent from foster homes to uncaring relatives and back to foster homes, having to start at a new school each time he moved. He cried as he told me about his failed therapies, years of psychoanalysis, years of screaming and beating pillows, of regressive therapies, dream analysis and anti-depressants. Although he had no motivation to meditate on his own, at each of our sessions I led him through the exercise of attuning to the pervasive space of fundamental consciousness. He often complained to me about the futility of this exercise, saying that he felt no lasting change from it.

Then, after eleven months, Paul's complaint changed. He told me sadly that he could both see and feel a kind of thickness, like 'thick water', in the space. I asked him to direct his focus within the thickness and to attune to its emotional quality. He was able to do this without difficulty and reported that it felt like sadness. He said that he now realized that this sadness had always been there since as far back as he could remember, but that he had never actually seen it before. I then asked him to just observe the thick sadness in the space, as we sat silently together. After about twenty minutes, Paul began to cry. It was not the steady drizzle of tears that almost always accompanied his speech, but deep sobs that opened his whole throat – the outraged, desperate wail of an abandoned child.

Since that session, Paul has been able to meditate on his own. He reports that the space of fundamental consciousness is becoming increasingly clear, and that he sometimes feels happiness in his body for no reason at all. Having visible, palpable evidence that sadness, although so familiar, is not really him but something that he has carried within himself, he has begun to take an interest in his own healing process.

The essential quality of emotion can be attuned to directly, or by accessing the subtle core of the chest. It can also be opened through devotional prayer and through service to others. Self-love and love for others deepen simultaneously in the spiritual dimension. Unconditional love is the essential nature of the whole relational field of self and other. It is the essential nature of both our internal contact with ourselves, and our mutual contact with other people.

PHYSICAL SENSATION

The essential quality of physical sensation is the aspect of fundamental consciousness that has been least mentioned as such in the traditional spiritual teachings. But physical sensation is an inseparable part of our own essential being and our oneness with other life. The realization of the essential quality of physical sensation is as necessary for spiritual maturity as the qualities of love and awareness.

Without the quality of physical sensation, our experience of the world lacks texture and tactile pleasure. Our intimacy with other people lacks sensual pleasure. And without this essential aspect of ourselves, our realization of fundamental consciousness is always fragmented. Our entire being is the instrument, or the vessel, of spiritual realization. If we keep part of this vessel closed, then we deprive ourselves of our full range of spiritual experience.

I believe that attention to physical sensation as part of spiritual realization is one of the most important aspects of the newly emerging spiritual understanding in the West. The use of ancient practices such as Tantric sexual techniques, drumming circles and some of the martial arts, cultivate physical sensation, as do various forms of movement therapy. We can also realize the essential quality of physical sensation by attuning to it directly within the pervasive space of fundamental consciousness, or by accessing the base of the subtle core of the body.

Over the years that I have been teaching Subtle Self Work, I have found that, in general, people have more difficulty attuning to the essential quality of physical sensation than to the emotion and awareness aspects of fundamental consciousness. Although they can access physical sensation within their bodies, they are familiar with only a minimal degree of this experience, and they have not felt nearly the depth of sensation that is available to them.

For many people, it is necessary to release defensive holding patterns and limiting beliefs about sexuality before they can attune to the spiritual dimension of physical sensation. Chapter seven addresses this important aspect of our spiritual oneness with other people. Here I will say briefly that, when people first discover the quality of physical sensation in themselves, it is often accompanied by a flush of embarrassment and guilt. Traditional religions, in presenting a sexually repressive code of behavior, have been responsible for much of our difficulty in attuning to physical sensation. The taboo against sensuality has very often been augmented in people's childhoods with the threat of God's anger and rejection, or even with Hell, creating a seemingly impassable barrier between physical sensation and spirituality. Even if our families did not hold these religious ideas, the vestiges of this misguided morality still linger in our culture, as a legacy of the fragmentation between our upper and lower bodies that is mirrored from one generation to the next. It persists as a deeply engrained, and often unconscious, belief that physical sensation is not as important or as noble an aspect of ourselves as the qualities of love and awareness.

However, there is really no way that we can disconnect physical sensation from love and awareness, any more than we can divide the blue tip of a candle flame from its orange base. To live in the spiritual dimension of life is to be able to truly enjoy ourselves in the innate and inseparable arenas of wisdom, love and sensual pleasure.

THE ESSENTIAL QUALITIES OF THE HUMAN FORM

We can experience the three essential qualities of fundamental consciousness pervading all forms in nature. In the human form we can distinguish a more delineated spectrum, where the qualities of physical sensation, emotion and awareness become, in our human anatomy, the qualities of gender, sexuality, power, love, voice and understanding. These are the qualities that are enfolded in our being, which deepen and develop as we realize fundamental consciousness. They are also the qualities of our self-expression, and our mutual contact with other human beings.

People are sometimes surprised that I include gender as a quality of fundamental consciousness. We each realize fundamental consciousness through subtle attunement to own our individual form. Therefore, even though it may seem strange to attribute gender to the spiritual dimension, fundamental consciousness is experienced in the human body as having the quality of gender of that particular body. Maleness is a slightly different quality from femaleness.

Some people have found this aspect of Subtle Self Work offensive to their sense of sexual politics. They want to think of themselves as 'gender-fluid', but they usually mean by this that they want to have access to a full range of personality traits and behaviors that have been culturally stereotyped as male or female. The ability to experience the quality of one's gender has nothing to do with limiting our personality in this way, nor does it dictate our choice of sexual partners. If we cannot experience the quality of our gender, it means that we are not inhabiting the genital and pelvic area of our body. This lack of attunement will diminish our contact with both ourselves and others. The quality of gender is particularly important to include in our self-attunement because it is an aspect of being that almost everyone constricts.

Wherever we are able to inhabit our body as fundamental consciousness, we gain the optimal functioning of that part of ourselves. In other words, as we inhabit our throat, we gain more use of our voice; as we inhabit our brain we gain more use of our mental faculties. Just as in the broader division of awareness, emotion and physical sensation, each of these qualities pervades our whole body.

DIRECT TRANSMISSION

Since no one is ever completely open to the spiritual dimension, there will be some areas of mutual contact and some areas of resistance and conflict even between two people who have realized fundamental consciousness. One of the ways in which relationships serve as a spiritual path is in helping the partners release the defenses that obstruct their realization of fundamental consciousness. An intimate relationship calls on our capacity for understanding, love and physical sensation. As we come to know and trust another person, the protective rigidities that we have created in ourselves are gradually surrendered. We are able to receive the stimulation of another person's emotion, awareness and sensation more and more deeply into our own being. Along with the development of trust, the mutual stimulation of awareness, emotion and physical sensation deepens both partners' realization of fundamental consciousness through a process that is known in Eastern traditions as 'direct transmission.'

Direct transmission usually refers to the relationship between spiritual teachers and their students. Just by being in the presence of a realized teacher, our own consciousness begins to resonate with the consciousness of the teacher. The extraordinary openness of a spiritual master can help to dissolve the holding patterns that obstruct our own realization. Many people have experienced, as I have, the phenomenon of their own heart softening in the powerful love of a spiritual teacher.

Direct transmission is actually a universal principle of human relationship, and occurs, to some degree, whenever two people interact. For example, if a woman is more attuned to the quality of awareness than her partner is, the relationship will increase her partner's attunement to the quality of awareness. This transmission happens automatically, as a result of the contact between two people, and in an ongoing relationship, the transmission will have a lasting effect.

There are many theories about what causes people to become attracted to each other. As attraction seems to be a very complex phenomenon, most of the theories are probably correct. Harville Hendrix[13] has popularized the idea that we are drawn to people who remind us of our parents, particularly in ways that caused us some emotional pain in our childhood. According to this theory, the operative force of the attraction is the innate desire to resolve the conflicts and heal the wounds that have created problems and deficits in our own being. In other words, we are drawn to the person who has the potential for helping us to grow.

I believe that another similar basis of attraction between sensitive people involves the pattern of openness to the essential qualities of fundamental consciousness. When one partner is more attuned to a quality than the other, there will be the direct transmission described above, as well as conflict and the potential for growth. Sensitive people are sometimes drawn to partners who are open in ways that they are not, through the same desire for growth and wholeness that motivates us on the psychological level. Even if this is not the basis of attraction, these differences in spiritual openness, and their resultant conflicts, can be regarded as opportunities to progress on the spiritual path.

---

13 Harville Hendrix, *Getting the Love You Want* (New York: Harper Perennial, 1988)

We are also attracted to people who are open in the same qualities that we are, because the degree of mutual contact in these areas makes a relationship satisfying and pleasurable. When two people are open in the same qualities, they can touch and see into each other deeply in those aspects of being. We feel both kinship and passion with a person who can meet us in the same depth that we know ourselves.

Our pattern of openness and defense is expressed continuously. It affects every aspect of our communication, including the quality of our touch, the expression in our eyes, the sound of our voice. If we listen carefully to people's speech, for example, we will hear where they are most open in their bodies. We can tell if they live mostly in their mental functioning, or in their emotions, or in physical sensation. The sound will also change with the content of the message, but there will be an underlying quality that does not change – except through psychological and spiritual growth – that reflects the personality of the speaker. These expressions of openness and defense give us a subtle or even subliminal knowledge of the other people in our lives.

EXERCISE 5
ATTUNING TO THE QUALITIES OF
FUNDAMENTAL CONSCIOUSNESS

Partners sit facing each other, either on cushions or chairs, with your backs straight. Both people follow the instructions at the same time.

Repeat the end of exercise 1: Feel that you are inside your whole body. Find the space outside your body. Experience that the space inside and outside your body is the same, continuous space. Experience that the space pervading your body also pervades your partner's body. (Remain in your own body, as you attune to the space that pervades you both.)

Now attune to the quality of awareness. This means to become aware that you are aware. You can attune to this quality in the upper third of your body and above your head.

Experience the quality of awareness pervading your whole body.

Attune to your own quality of awareness and your partner's quality of awareness at the same time.

Attune to the quality of emotion. You will probably notice that you automatically move your attention down to the middle third of your body as you attune to the quality of emotion.

Experience the quality of emotion pervading your whole body.

Attune to your own quality of emotion and your partner's quality of emotion at the same time.

Attune to the quality of physical sensation. You can attune to this quality in the bottom third of your torso and legs. Bring your attention as far down in your torso and legs, and as deeply into the quality of physical sensation as you can.

Experience that the quality of physical sensation pervades your whole body.

Attune to your own quality of physical sensation and your partner's quality of physical sensation at the same time.

Now attune to the qualities of awareness and physical sensation at the same time, as they pervade your whole body. Bring in the quality of emotion as well, pervading your whole body.

Attune to all three qualities in yourself and your partner at the same time.

Sit with your partner in this rich space of awareness, emotion and physical sensation. Let your breath pass smoothly and evenly through the space of your own body, without disturbing your attunement to the awareness, emotion and physical sensation of fundamental consciousness.

EXERCISE 6
ATTUNING TO THE ESSENTIAL QUALITIES
OF THE HUMAN FORM

Partners sit facing each other on cushions or chairs, with your backs straight. Both people follow the instructions at the same time.

This exercise can also be practiced in the yab yum position, in which (for heterosexual couples) the woman sits on the man's lap, facing him. This can be practiced sitting cross-legged, with the woman's legs wrapped around the man's pelvis, but it is easier sitting in a chair.

Begin by focusing on your breath, until the breath is calm and even. The inhale and exhale should be the same duration.

Feel that you are inside your feet and legs; that you inhabit your feet and legs.

Feel that you are inside your pelvis; that you inhabit your pelvis. Attune to the quality of your gender inside your pelvis. Bring your breath down into your pelvis and let it pass through the quality of your gender.

Attune to the quality of your gender and your partner's gender at the same time.

Feel that you inhabit your mid-section, between your pelvis and ribs, including the solar plexus area beneath your ribs. Attune to the quality of your power, your personal strength, inside your mid-section. Bring your breath down into your mid-section and let it pass through the quality of power.

Attune to your own quality of power and your partner's quality of power at the same time.

Feel that you are inside your chest. Attune to the quality of love inside your chest. Bring your breath down into your chest and let it pass through the quality of love.

Attune to your own quality of love and your partner's quality of love at the same time.

Feel that you are inside your shoulders, arms and hands.

Feel that you are inside your neck, from behind your mouth down to the collarbones. Attune to the quality of your own voice, your potential to speak, inside your neck. Bring your breath down through your neck and let it pass through the quality of your voice.

Attune to your quality of voice and your partner's quality of voice at the same time.

Feel that you are inside your head, and inside your whole face.

Feel that you are inside your brain, both hemispheres of your brain. Attune to the quality of your understanding inside your whole brain. Bring your breath through your brain and let it pass through the quality of understanding.

Attune to your own quality of understanding and your partner's quality of understanding at the same time.

For advanced spiritual practitioners: attune to the space above your head. (There is no attunement to a particular quality for this space.) Attune to the space above your own head and above your partner's head at the same time.

Feel that you are inside your whole body at once. Experience that you are one unified being inside your body. Attune to the quality of Self inside your whole body. Bring your breath into your whole body and let it pass through the quality of Self.

Attune to your own quality of Self and your partner's quality of Self at the same time.

Note: Please remember that these attunements are exercises for stretching the essential qualities. Do not hold on to these qualities when you have finished the exercise. Let yourself settle into your natural state.

EXERCISE 7
TOUCHING WITH THE ESSENTIAL QUALITIES

This exercise can be practiced either sitting or lying down next to each other.

Rest your hands on each other's hands, with your palms touching each other's palms.

Inhabit your pelvis. Attune to the quality of gender inside your pelvis. Touch each other's hands with the quality of gender. (You may feel that the quality you are attuning to in your body automatically affects the quality of your touch.)

Inhabit your mid-section, between your ribs and your pelvis. Attune to the quality of power inside your mid-section. Touch each other's hands with the quality of power.

Inhabit your chest. Attune to the quality of love inside your chest. Touch each other's hands with the quality of love.

Inhabit your neck. Attune to the quality of your voice. Touch each other's hands with the quality of your voice.

Inhabit your whole brain. Attune to the quality of your understanding. Touch each other's hands with the quality of your understanding.

Inhabit your whole body. Attune to the quality of self in your whole body. Touch each other's hands with the quality of self.

CHAPTER FIVE

Bare Perception

*The mountains, rivers, earth, grasses and trees are always
emanating a subtle, precious light, day and night,
always emanating a subtle precious sound, demonstrating
and expounding to all people the unsurpassed truth.*

Yuan-sou

In 1981, while living at a Zen monastery in upstate New
York, I met a Yugoslav musician named Zoran, who is now
my husband. One of the things that attracted me to him was
a quality of alert silence that seemed to surround him like a
field of radar. In one of our first encounters, we were sitting
on a bench at the edge of the forest, just as the crickets began
their evening uproar. With our heads in close proximity, my
hearing was stretched open by his sensitivity to sound. The
insects' brassy song became an exquisite pattern of tiny
discernible distances.

In the previous chapters I have described how our capacities
for awareness, love and physical sensation deepen and unify as
we realize spiritual oneness. As our subjective organization –
our defenses and other holding patterns – of these capacities
dissolves, so does our sense of being a subject separate from an
objective external world. Our own being is experienced as
continuous with the unified awareness, love and physical
sensation that pervades everything. This same transformation
occurs in our senses. As we realize spiritual oneness, our
perception becomes more subtle and unified. As our manipulation of our perception dissolves, we realize that there is no
true separation between subject and object, that there is no

boundary between ourselves as the perceiver and that which we perceive. All of our perceptions arise directly out of the unified empty space of fundamental consciousness. In the spiritual literature of the East, this clear immediacy of the perceptible world is called 'direct' or 'bare' perception. An early Buddhist text describes bare perception thus: 'In the seen there will be just the seen; in the heard, just the heard; in smelling, tasting, touching, just smelling, tasting, touching; in the cognized, just the cognized.'[14]

In the West, this aspect of spiritual realization has often been described as a dropping away of veils. It feels as if there is finally no barrier between ourselves and whatever we are perceiving. We are fully alert to the present moment – just as it is. This stripped-clean perception reveals a very different world than the one we used to know. The apparent solidity of our environment now appears to be transparent, permeable. This means that instead of seeing and touching just the surface of the people and things around us, we can see and touch through their internal depth. We can look at a flower and see the vibrancy of the life force within it. We can touch a person and feel the qualities of that person's being within their body.

As our perception becomes more subtle, we are able to perceive the luminosity and the qualities of aliveness and sentience that pervade the whole material world. Everything that we perceive appears to be radiant, and both substantial and weightless at the same time, as if it were made of consciousness. Recently, on the last morning of a week-long Subtle Self Work retreat, one of the participants came to the session very excited. He had been casually looking out of a restaurant window at the forest as he ate breakfast. There was a telephone pole right next to a tree. He noticed, for the first

---

14 Bhikkhu Nanananda, *Concept and Reality in Early Buddhist Thought* (Kandy, Sri Lanka: Buddhist Publication Society, 1971), p.30

time in his life, how very much more alive the tree was than the telephone pole. In the spiritual dimension, even a blade of grass looks conscious, as if it could think and speak.

Eastern metaphysics says that each sense is a type of consciousness. We do not perceive the world with the sense organs alone; our consciousness perceives the world through the organs of the senses. It is really our consciousness that sees, for example; the eyes are just the instrument of seeing. We can say that the eyes are like the lens of a camera; they do not actually take the picture. As we realize spiritual oneness, we discover that our various sense consciousnesses are actually the one fundamental consciousness that pervades everything. The revered ninth century Zen Master Rinzai said, 'O Brethren, the Mind-Reality has no definite form. It permeates and runs through the whole universe. In the eye, it acts as sight; in the ear it acts as hearing; in the nose it acts as the sense of smell; in the mouth it speaks; in the hand it grasps; in the foot it walks.'[15]

As fundamental consciousness, all of our senses function together. Just as we are able to think and feel at the same time, we are able to see and hear at the same time. Each moment occurs as a single, multi-faceted vibrational pattern that registers in all of our senses at once. Just like the movement of our thoughts, feelings and physical sensations, our perceptions register in the stillness of fundamental consciousness without altering it. In the language of Zen, they 'leave no trace". The sound of a gong, for example, can reverberate through the stillness and silence of our consciousness without disturbing the stillness or silence at all. This means that the reverberation will occur in its totality, without any interference on our own part.

Bare perception is entirely effortless. We do not have to look in order to see, or to listen in order to hear. We need only

15 Toshihiko Izutsu, *Toward a Philosophy of Zen Buddhism* (Boulder, CO: Prajna Press, 1982), p.39

to receive our environment exactly as it is in each moment.

The spiritual dimension of perception has all the same functions and qualities of other aspects of fundamental consciousness. For example, direct transmission occurs in perception just as it does in the qualities of awareness, love and physical sensation. As I described above, in my encounter with my future husband, the openness of another person's perception can stretch open our own. This can happen when we see or hear a work of art. If we open to the depth and harmony of the artist's perception, we may release some of the holding patterns that limit our own capacity for perception.

The senses are also pathways of resonance and mutual contact between ourselves and other life. We make 'eye contact' with other people, for example. And when we touch another person, we experience mutual tactile contact between that person's body and our own. This form of contact becomes increasingly subtle and pleasurable as we realize spiritual oneness. Just as two people can experience the resonance and continuity of love, awareness or physical sensation that pervades them both, so they can open to oneness through their gaze, or through any of the senses. In this practice, the function of direct transmission will help both partners release the holding patterns that obstruct their perception.

Perception can function as a path towards spiritual realization in the same way that love, awareness or physical sensation can. The Buddha is said to have attained his complete enlightenment when, after sitting for many days absorbed in meditation, he opened his eyes and saw the morning star.

Since fundamental consciousness pervades our whole being, to perceive with (or as) fundamental consciousness means that we perceive with our whole being. We see, hear, touch, taste and smell with our whole body and mind. Several years ago I attended a meditation intensive with the Zen Master Joshu

Sasaki Roshi. In the private interviews with him, he tested the student's degree of enlightenment by banging a short wooden stick on the ground, as he wanted to see if we could open to the full impact of the sound. There are many stories in Zen Buddhism in which a master is asked to define enlightenment and answers, 'plum blossoms in the snow', or something of that sort. Enlightenment is whatever we are experiencing in the moment, experienced with our whole being.

It is important to know that our perception shifts towards this unified, direct and effortless experience as we realize fundamental consciousness. Otherwise, we may spend many wonderful hours shut away in meditation and then return to our fragmented state of consciousness as soon as we encounter the perceptual stimulation of our everyday lives.

However, some spiritual teachers place so much emphasis on bare perception that we might conclude that spiritual realization involves only the perceptual aspect of our being. I have observed many spiritual practitioners attempting to live only in the clarity of their perception while their capacity for emotion, for example, remains constricted. Although we are never entirely without constriction, to focus only on one aspect of spiritual realization will intensify the fragmentation in our being.

Spiritual practitioners, having been particularly sensitive as children, often grow up with exactly this imbalance of focus towards the external world. The vividness of the sights and sounds around them, and the changes in facial expression, vocal tone and other emotional cues from the people in their environment, distract many sensitive children from inward contact with their own emotions, thoughts and physical sensations. It is then only too easy to continue to fine-tune this perceptual vigilance through spiritual practice. However we cannot actually arrive at the fullness of bare perception without opening all of the capacities of our being.

UNVEILING THE SENSES

There are many ways in which we limit or veil our perception. One of the main obstacles to bare perception is the tendency to substitute ideas for experience itself. These concepts come, for the most part, out of our past experience. Human beings are fast learners. As children, we learn that life is a certain way, that men and women and all of the various objects around us are a certain way – based on the information that first impresses itself on our minds. It is very challenging for us as adults, having learned how life is, to perceive each moment of life unfolding anew.

Our familiarity with the idea of 'table', for example, obscures our actual experience of this particular table in this present moment. In order to truly experience the table, we need to receive it, without any preconception, in the clear, empty space of our consciousness. When this occurs, we realize that the table is not separate from the consciousness that reveals it, that it is not separate from our perception. Our own existence and the table's existence appear to arise simultaneously out of the same consciousness.

To perceive another human being in this way is particularly challenging, and important, in ongoing relationships. Over time we tend to form an idea of who the other person is and then expect them to be that way forever. We form habitual ways of relating to people based on our static mental idea of who they are. When we receive our partner or friend in the unguarded openness of bare perception, however, our relationship with them is constantly renewed.

When our senses are constricted, it is easy to feel withdrawn from the limited world we perceive, or to project onto it our old fears and aversions. To feel truly involved with other people, we need to truly perceive them. We need to allow ourselves to hear the sound of their voices, feel the quality of their touch, observe the expressions and attitudes that change in them from moment to moment.

Mental concepts also impede our innate function of attraction. We possess a natural capacity for arousal in our intelligence, emotions and sexuality that draws us towards particular people. Our images of the perfect man or woman can prevent us from finding a mate, by obstructing our ability to respond to the actual people we encounter. These images are often based on our personal history. I worked with a woman who always rejected men whose hands looked 'too smooth'. Until she examined her childhood, she had not associated this rather limiting preference with her grandfather, a hard-working carpenter who had been the only positive male figure in her early years.

Our images of male and female attractiveness also emerge from the communal, cultural fantasy that is passed from one generation to the next, and reinforced through the media. Cultural images are difficult to shed because they are ubiquitous, and become as unnoticeable as background noise. To rid ourselves of these generic images of men and women requires that we allow the people in our lives to register fully in our perception. When our senses are open, we often find beauty where we did not expect it.

When we project mental concepts onto the people and things around us, we live in an abstract world. Interestingly, the realization of the spiritual dimension is a progression away from abstraction and towards an experience of specific, concrete reality. Spiritual realization is a realization of this present moment, fully lived, just as it is.

Besides the projection of concepts onto reality, we limit our perception by simply not being attentive to the moment. Anyone who has attempted to sit and quiet the mind in meditation for any prolonged period is familiar with the many ways in which we divert our attention from the present. For the most part, these ways are habitual patterns of distraction that we have cultivated all through our lives in order to cope with anxiety and boredom. We also economize our attention in order to concentrate on particular tasks, like the person who dims the perceptual world in order to think without distraction, and we automatically blot out unpleasant perceptual stimuli. Over time, these fragmented or narrowed patterns of focus become fixed in the tissues of the sense organs. This often produces a vicious cycle in which we increase the rigidity of our focus in order to compensate for limitation or exhaustion in our sense organs.

Holding patterns in the sense organs can become so severe that they cause deafness or blindness. Meir Schneider, a man who was born blind, writes a moving account of his partial recovery of vision through relaxation exercises, and through deep insight into his fear of seeing.[16] There are many reasons why people are afraid to encounter the world with clear perception. Schneider discovered that he was terrified that other people would not see what he saw, that vision would isolate him from other human beings. Some people fear that they will dislike what they see, if they allow themselves to see clearly; or that they will be distracted by desire for the people and objects around them.

We created most of the rigid limitations in our perception as children, to defend ourselves against the impact of specific painful perceptual stimuli. We may, for example, shut out the sound of our parents arguing by constricting our hearing, or shut down our sense of smell against a persistent odor of whisky that accompanies strange alterations in our parents'

---

16 Meir Schneider, Self Healing: *My Life and Vision* (New York, NY: Routledge & Kegan Paul, 1987)

behavior. We may respond to spoken or unspoken commands not to perceive something, coming from adults who wish to conceal themselves from the direct scrutiny of children. We also match the ways our parents limit their own perception by mirroring their holding patterns in our own sense organs. As adults, we may guard against fully seeing the facial expressions of the people around us, because we unconsciously fear the same expression of anger, or neediness, for example that distorted our parents' features, or the same dissonance between vocal tone and facial expression that confused us as children.

HOW OUR PATTERN OF DEFENSE SHAPES OUR PERCEPTION

In addition to these direct defenses against perception, our sense organs are also constricted by the pattern of defense in our whole body. As I explained in the last chapter, each small part of ourselves contains the spectrum of our essential qualities (awareness/emotion/physical sensation), as well as the pattern of defense within our whole organism. If we are most open in our mental capacity and most defended in our physical sensation, for example, each of our senses will contain the same pattern of openness at the top – the top of the eyes, the top of the orifices of the ears, the top of the nostril orifices (towards the tip of the nose) – and constriction at the bottom.

Although this correspondence occurs in all of our senses, it is easiest to discern in our eyes. If we look carefully at other people, we will notice that we all gaze more through some parts of our eyes than others. If we have more internal contact with our head than our pelvis, for example, we will see more out of the top of our eyes than the bottom. This will produce a different expression in our eyes than in the eyes of someone who is more open in their pelvis or chest. Although this placement will change somewhat in different circumstances, most of these patterns of openness and defense are either habitual attitudes or chronic rigidities in the physical tissues of our body. In this way, we maintain specific limitations in our perception of our environment, which we mistake for the nature of reality.

The pattern of openness and defense in our sense organs determines the range of qualities in the world we perceive. If we see mostly through the top of our eyes, our visual perception of the world will lack texture and weight. You can try this out yourself by looking at the texture of the carpet in your room or the texture of the fabric of your clothes. If you observe yourself carefully as you do this, you will notice that you automatically gaze through the bottom of your eyes, and contact the bottom of your body, in order to do so.

Our holding patterns also determine the range of qualities in our sense organ contact; in our eye contact, for example, or our touch. If we constrict our emotional capacity, for example, there will be a corresponding lack of emotion in the expressiveness of our eyes or our touch, in our visual or tactile contact with other life. We will not be able to see or to touch 'from our heart'. The information that we receive through our senses will be limited in the same way.

As we realize spiritual oneness, the holding patterns in our senses gradually dissolve and we begin to receive the 'whole picture'. We are able to rest in the balance of internal and external experience, and the world around us becomes increasingly vivid and meaningful. There is a mysterious and satisfying harmony in the 'multi-media' experience of each moment.

The process of freeing the senses can be even more

challenging than letting go of other types of holding patterns, because it actually changes the world in which we live. The new range of information available to us may require that we re-examine our life choices. There may also be some temporary blurring of perception as we release our habitual ways of focusing, but that will dissolve into greater clarity. Some people also find it difficult to adjust to the luminosity of bare perception. I worked with one woman who would emerge from meditation waving her hands in front of her as if to disperse the excess radiance in the air, and it took about a year before she became accustomed to the light-filled space as the normal appearance of the world.

It can also be difficult to shift from our abstract, imagined world to the stripped-down world of actual experience. Although I was a dancer for most of my childhood and adolescence, I experienced the main locus of my being high up in my head. From there I perceived the world around me as a moving array of symbolic meaning. Then, when I was in my twenties, a back injury forced me to enter into deeper contact with my body and self. One of the first things I noticed as I began the shift towards wholeness, was that the world seemed very different. It had become more solid, more soberly 'just the facts' in its look and sound and feel. Although some people feel lighter as they open to the spiritual dimension, I felt heavier, and everything around me suddenly had more substance and weight as well. I was struck by the ungraspable otherness of the world, for it was no longer tied up with my own imagination. Then, as I continued on my path, the appearance of the world also continued to change. The solidity of the world became transparent. There was a creek near my home in upstate New York where I often went to meditate. Sitting there one day I noticed that the rocks seemed weightless, that they were both substantial and 'empty' at the same time. They appeared to be made of radiant space.

A friend once told me sadly that, after many years on his spiritual path, he was still unable to see God in everyone. My understanding is that God is in the seeing itself. As our own vision becomes the subtle, bare perception of fundamental consciousness, it sees itself in all of the beings and objects we encounter.

Another woman, who works as a practitioner of cranial-sacral therapy (a subtle form of bodywork), told me that she had met a photographer who travels around the world trying to take pictures of divine light. She said that she felt she understood this photographer because her own work with people requires her to touch the divine light in the body. All of our senses can become subtle enough to detect the radiance of the spiritual dimension in other people, no matter how hidden it is. In his 'Song to Naropa', the Tibetan Buddhist sage Tilopa calls this 'gazing with sheer awareness into sheer awareness'.[17]

SEEING THROUGH THE BODY

As we realize fundamental consciousness, we gain the ability to 'see-feel' through the internal space of another person's body. We can perceive, within this space, the qualities that make up their being, the streaming of energy through their body, and even the movement of their feelings and thoughts. Some very sensitive people can hear a person's unspoken thoughts. Some can see the internal organs in people's bodies which enables them to diagnose illnesses.

Just as we do not need to see a person's facial expression in order to detect the quality of anger or sadness in their voice, so we are able to perceive emotional qualities in the body. We

17 Lex Hixon, *Mother of the Buddhas* (Wheaton, Illinios: Quest Books, 1993) pp.246-247

can discern both a person's present emotional responses, and the static emotional qualities that have been held in their body since childhood. Interestingly, we do not even need to be in proximity to someone in order to be able to read their emotional responses. For example, in telephone conversations we can often perceive the emotional reactions of the person we are speaking with in the silence that precedes their verbal response.

Bare perception is thus an inseparable part of our oneness and intimacy with other life. Although many people are afraid at first of what their increased perception will reveal, most find that it brings them a deep sense of kinship with other living beings. When we perceive another person this intimately, we are able to recognize in them the same innate spirit and the same painful constraints that we know in ourselves. This is an unshakable foundation for compassion. It also makes our relationships less confusing because we can see more clearly where people are open and where they are defended. In other words, we can see 'where they are coming from'. As well as clarifying our connection to the people in our lives at present, this clear-through perception can help us resolve important relationships from our past.

A woman named Cynthia came to work with me because she had become obsessed with a man who had left her several months before. She felt compelled to keep calling him, only to be rejected again and again. I was impressed by Cynthia's attractive, lively spirit and I sympathized with her frustration that she was directing her considerable passion towards a man who was not interested in her. As she narrated for me her history of relationships over the past twenty years of her adult life, however, it became clear that she was consistently drawn to men who rejected her. As she was well read in the field of psychology, she was able to acknowledge that this pattern might have something to do with her relationship with her father.

During one session I placed an empty chair opposite Cynthia and asked her to picture her father sitting on it. The empty chair technique comes from gestalt therapy and is very effective for releasing bound emotions relating to important people in our lives. However I wanted Cynthia to do something more subtle than the usual gestalt-style dialogue. I wanted her to really see her father, to see through his body to the life within. She stared at the empty chair, seeming to shrink in her own skin. 'Can you see him there?' I asked. 'Yes.' Her expressive face had taken on a pathetic quality, like a beggar's. 'What do you feel when you look at him?' She sat with this question for a while, trying to articulate a feeling that she was so familiar with, but had never named. 'I feel locked out', she said finally.

I led Cynthia through the basic Subtle Self Work exercise for attuning to the clear space pervading her body and the environment. I asked her to experience the space pervading her body also pervading the image of her father's body, sitting on the empty chair. 'This subtle, pervasive consciousness,' I told her, 'is the basis of perception. Just as your consciousness pervades your father's body, so does your perception.'

Cynthia was surprised to find that she could see through her father's body. I asked her to describe his chest, and she sat for several moments in fundamental consciousness with her father, focusing on his chest. I watched her expression register surprise, then understanding, and then sadness. 'There is a stillness there', she said without turning away from him, 'a kind of thickness.' I asked her to focus her attention within the thickness itself, and then to 'see-feel' the emotional tone inside the thickness. I watched Cynthia tune even more subtly and precisely into the imaginary figure on the chair. Then she began to cry. 'There is fear in there, it is almost terror', she said, 'and also longing, the same longing that I feel for him. But the fear covers it.'

Cynthia felt relieved by this perception. She had always assumed that her father did not like her, that he shut her out because he found her deficient in some way. She had tried to make herself more worthy of his approval, but her efforts had never won his love. Now she could see, with her own eyes, that it was his difficulty, his own fear, that kept him from expressing love for her.

Cynthia sat for a while longer with the image of her father in the chair. She practiced being with him without making herself smaller, or holding her breath. She let herself feel the longing in her own chest and in her father's chest, and recognize that his inability to love her was not a personal rejection of her. This would help her begin to let go of the need to try and win his love. It would also help her let go of the compulsion to replay this confusing, painful relationship with the men in her life.

When we see people clearly, we cease to perceive them as generic types, or to respond to them in a way that is based on our associations with generic types of people. For example, people who feel insecure about their own intelligence might classify anyone with an advanced education as an 'intellectual' and proceed to relate to them with fear and resentment. Bare perception means that we allow each person we encounter to register in our senses in all of their complexity and uniqueness. We experience and respond to them directly, as they appear to us at that moment, without preconceptions.

We are also able to see through the distorted images that people project of themselves. We can distinguish fantasy from actuality, sentimentality from love, inflation from power or provocative posturing from true sexuality. When we are able to see beyond these images we can no longer be manipulated by them, and we lose our fear of them.

I worked with a woman who was preparing herself for a confrontation with her ex-husband concerning the care of their teenaged daughter. Suzanne described her husband as a very powerful man. She knew that she would have to fight for what she wanted, but she was afraid that he would easily overpower her.

I gave Suzanne the same exercise that I had done with Cynthia, placing an empty chair across from her and asking her to attune to fundamental consciousness pervading both her and an image of her ex-husband seated there. Suzanne had great difficulty picturing her ex-husband in the chair, as she was afraid to look at him, even in her imagination. She could only picture him there if she herself turned sideways away from him, but she was unable to face him, which made her even more agitated about her impending meeting with him.

I told Suzanne to dissolve the image of her ex-husband and, instead, I sat down in the chair facing her. I asked her to attune to fundamental consciousness pervading both herself and me. Then I instructed her to bring her focus into the mid-section of her body, between her pelvis and her ribs, and to inhabit that part of her body as deeply and fully as she could. When she had done this, I asked her to attune to the quality of power in her mid-section. Carefully, and with a self-deprecating inclination of her head, she let herself feel the quality of power in her mid-section. Next I asked her to see-feel the same quality of power inside my mid-section and, to her amazement, she was able to do this too.

Then I entered into a battle of power with her, increasing the intensity of the power in my body – we have a volume control on all of these qualities – and asking her to match or better me with the intensity of her own power. Suzanne proved to be quite good at this game. She straightened her head and matched me belly for belly until we were two very powerful women facing each other.

To an onlooker, it would have seemed that we were both seated very peacefully and at ease, not interacting with each other. However, the true power in the body is very effective with other people. In fact it is much stronger than the pretense of power that most intimidating people display. To demonstrate this to Suzanne, I inflated my upper body into the image that most of us associate with the powerful, or overpowering, person. It is the image of a bully. Suzanne quickly turned away from me. 'That's just what he looks like', she said with her face still averted.

'I'm going to hold this pose', I told her, 'and you see if you can face me again, and tune back into your real power.' Suzanne followed these directions slowly, and I waited until she was again the powerful woman who had played matching mid-sections with me. 'Now', I said, holding myself in the inflated attitude, 'make sure that you are attuned to fundamental consciousness pervading both yourself and me. And let yourself really see me, all the way through my body.' As Suzanne did this, I felt her regain her sense of power and ease. 'What do you see?', I asked. 'There is no power in you', she said. 'It is only muscular tension holding an attitude. There is no power in your body.'

All of the genuine qualities of our being are expressed effortlessly, without our having to impress them upon other people. In fact, they only emerge when we let go of our manipulation of ourselves and others. When we experience people in the clear space of fundamental consciousness, we can easily discern the layering of images and attitudes that obscure essential being.

Sometimes people try to restrain their perception as it becomes more subtle so as not to be intrusive towards other people. As I described in chapter two, we can invade another person's 'space' by projecting our focus and energy into their body. However, the bare perception of fundamental consciousness does not involve any projecting of ourselves into other people. In fact, the more we inhabit our own body, the more subtle our perception becomes. Bare perception is the natural and inevitable result of spiritual oneness. We cannot suppress our perception without limiting our own maturity. We can, of course, refrain from being intrusive in the way we relate with other people, which often means keeping one's observations to oneself. It is also good to keep in mind that we are never without any subjective coloration, so however clear our perception seems to us, it must still be considered our own personal view.

I have found, however, that we usually feel great relief when we are clearly perceived, even if the actual content of the perception is not verbalized. When someone sees us deeply and compassionately it can help us see ourselves with the same degree of insight and acceptance. This is one of the most healing factors in the relationship between therapist and client, or between spiritual teacher and student. It is also one of the most healing functions of intimate relationships.

EXERCISE 8
BARE PERCEPTION

A – Begin by attuning to fundamental consciousness: feel that you are inside all of your body at once. Find the space outside your body. Experience that the space inside and outside your body is the same, continuous space; it pervades you.

Experience that the space which pervades your body also pervades the walls of the room and everything in the room. Be sure to remain within your own body as you experience this.

Let yourself hear all the sounds in your environment. Experience that the pervasive space is doing the hearing. You do not have to listen in order to hear; the sounds simply occur in the space. The sounds are changing vibrational patterns that occur in the space without altering the space in any way. In other words, the space remains motionless as the sounds move through it. Even subtle 'white noise', like the electrical hum in the house, is pervaded by the space. You are hearing with your whole self; your whole body and mind.

Now experience that the pervasive space is doing the seeing. Let your own visual field dissolve and become one with fundamental consciousness. You do not have to look in order to see; all of the visual images will appear in the space without any effort on your part. Just like the sounds, they are vibrational patterns that occur in the space without changing the space in any way. It is helpful to practice this with moving objects, such as leaves moving in the wind, or a flickering candle flame. Let the movement occur while remaining in the motionless expanse of your consciousness. You are seeing with your whole body and mind.

Now let yourself see and hear at the same time. Again the sounds and visual stimuli occur and move through the absolute stillness of your consciousness. Let yourself receive these patterns in your consciousness just as they are.

B – Now sit facing your partner. Experience that the space pervading your own body also pervades the body of your partner. Be careful to remain within your own body as you attune to the space pervading both of you.

Allow yourself to perceive your partner with the pervasive space of fundamental consciousness. Do not focus on any specific part or aspect of your partner, but let your partner register as a whole in the open space of your consciousness. Experience that fundamental consciousness pervades and reflects all of the vibrational patterns that make up the appearance, sounds, smells, emotions, thoughts and sensations of your partner.

EXERCISE 9
SEEING THROUGH THE BODY

Sit facing your partner. Your partner can keep his or her eyes closed. Again, feel that you are inside your whole body all at once. Find the space outside your body. Experience that the space inside and outside your body is the same, continuous space. Now experience that the space which pervades your body also pervades the body of your partner. You are both pervaded by the same space of fundamental consciousness.

Bring your attention to the space pervading your partner's head. Be sure to stay attuned to the space pervading your whole body and the whole body of your partner as you do this. Do not project your focus into your partner's head.

Let yourself see/feel/hear the internal space of your partner's head. See if you can experience where your partner is more open and where they are more defended within their head. (Some people live more on the left, others more on the right side of their head; some inhabit the crown of their head more than the base of their skull, or vice versa.) Now let yourself perceive the quality of your partner's intelligence, which will feel something like the quality of your own intelligence, but not exactly the same.

*Bring your attention to the space pervading your partner's chest.
Again, do not project your focus into your partner's chest. Let
the pervasive space itself do the seeing. Let yourself see/feel/hear
the internal space of your partner's chest. Again, you will, with
practice, be able to discern where your partner is closed or open
in their chest, and the particular quality of their love. You will
also be able to feel the qualities of any emotions that may be
held in their chest, such as childhood sadness or chronic anxiety.*

*You can repeat this exercise with your partner's mid-section and
pelvis.*

A word of caution: if you are just beginning in your practice
of seeing through the body, or if you do not know your
partner well, I suggest that you do not reveal to them what
you see in their body. Even if you are right, they may not be
ready to use the information constructively.

Partners can take turns being the one who does the seeing
and the one who is seen. When both partners feel comfortable
with this subtle perception, you can practice seeing within
each other at the same time.

CHAPTER SIX

Compassion

'But one man loved the pilgrim soul in you,
And loved the sorrows of your changing face.'
William Butler Yeats, *'When You Are Old'*

Compassion is one of the primary lessons of the spiritual path. It is through the awakening of compassion that we are able to feel genuine concern for the well-being of everyone we encounter, and for all of nature. Through compassion we are able to abandon our own agendas; we are able to listen and respond with an open heart and a clear mind in all of our interactions. We become conduits for the spontaneous unfolding of circumstances towards healing and growth.

Compassion is essential for intimate relationships. It allows us to love in the face of imperfection and obstruction. It allows us to love that which is different from our own personality. It allows us to love even when our own expectations and desires are not being satisfied. And it helps us to accept the needs and changes that occur as our partner continues to grow; to love and honor our partner's 'pilgrim soul'. Since we cannot be truly intimate with another person without the element of compassion, intimate relationships can be powerful vehicles for developing this crucial aspect of spiritual maturity.

COMPASSION FOR THE WOUNDED CHILD

All relationships have problems, and they are usually the problems that we most need to face for our own growth. We are often most attracted to a partner who fits the specific rifts in our relationships with the people we loved and depended upon in our childhood. Through compassion for both ourselves and our partner we can heal this rift; we can dissolve the barriers that have limited our contact with ourselves and other people.

As a therapist working with couples, I have seen countless examples of the healing power of compassion. When Lenny and Sarah first came to work with me, they wanted me to help them separate. Lenny explained to me that after six months of living together it was clear to them that they were 'incompatible', but they could not bring themselves to actually part. They sat at opposite ends of the couch in my office, with Sarah looking cool, contained and determined, and Lenny expressing outrage in the restless movements of his arms and legs. 'It's just sick that I'm still with this guy,' Sarah began and Lenny, without missing a beat, came back with, 'She's sick all right.' Sitting across from them, though, it seemed to me that the tension in the space between them on the couch contained more sadness and longing than animosity. I suggested to them that their conflicted state might be a sign of potential growth in their relationship, rather than separation. Lenny looked somewhat hopeful at this, but Sarah disagreed immediately. 'Lenny is verbally abusive towards me', she said with finality, 'I won't allow him to abuse me anymore.'

Over the next few weeks, Sarah described Lenny's relentless sarcasm towards her. Lenny complained that Sarah couldn't 'take it', that she would simply collapse in tears rather than standing up to him. Sarah's tears infuriated him. He felt that she was manipulating him into feeling bad about himself. He responded by becoming even more abusive towards her, so that the relationship went into an endless cycle, like a snake biting its own tail.

Then one session, when this pattern had become quite clear

to all of us, Sarah suddenly had a memory of her father hitting her. Sarah's father had died when she was six. Up to that point, she had described him to me as warm and playful, although she had an unusual scarcity of memories about him, and about her early childhood in general. Now she had an image of his face contorted in rage and the memory of his large hand slapping her face. As she described this, Sarah began to tremble with fear, and to bring her hands up protectively to her face. The gesture brought the memory into sharper focus. 'He's telling me not to talk back to him', she said, 'to never, ever talk back to him.' Sarah began to cry softly, as if still afraid to make any noise, and Lenny quietly slid towards her on the couch and put his arm around her shoulders.

In that session, Lenny understood why Sarah responded to his anger with tears. As a result, he began to relate to her with far more care. He also understood that Sarah's tears were not a cold manipulation of him, but a genuine reaction to his behavior. In the weeks that followed, Sarah also had a chance to see the source of Lenny's anger, and to become acquainted with the wounded little boy who had suffered the same abuse from his father that he now directed towards her. This made her less afraid of Lenny, and she found that she could stand up to him, and to talk back when he was sarcastic with her, because she had seen that he was as vulnerable as herself. This not only brought Sarah and Lenny closer to each other, it also helped them both heal some of their deepest psychological wounds.

To experience intimacy with another human being, we need, first of all, to feel compassion for the poignant, universal drama of a child's innocent expectation of love – in a world where love is almost always caged within a labyrinth of defenses. As young children, we created our own labyrinth of defenses, attitudes and beliefs in order to accomplish the task of finding love and recognition within the intricate mazes of our parents' hearts. We need to understand our present relationship as the interface of two labyrinths that have been carried forward from childhood. We may find that we have not only sympathy, but even admiration, for the struggles of both our partner and ourselves as we persist through the winding corridors of disappointment, loss, terror, and outrage, towards the possibility of intimacy.

The walls of these labyrinths are made of memory, phantom structures relevant only to the past. The power of these unconscious memories dissipates when they are exposed to our present-day consciousness, acceptance and love. Just as it is important for our own growth to know our own personal history, so it greatly facilitates intimate relationships for the partners to know each other's history. Psychological maturity is achieved through healing and releasing the memories of childhood wounds that are bound in our mind, energy and body. In an intimate relationship, we need to bring the same liberating force of love and acceptance to the wounded child that is bound in the mind and body of our partner. The recognition of the influence of the past on our partner's present-day behavior, even when our partner becomes the specter of our own deepest pain, can help us view his or her behavior with compassion, and open the path to love.

Whenever we become closely involved with another person, the possibility of love brings our unfulfilled childhood needs clamoring to the surface. If we were angry towards our original source of love, if we needed to protect ourselves from rejection or abuse, if we had to suppress our own identity for the sake of love – whatever our childhood situation – we will attempt to mold our new relationship to fit the original template so that we can at last resolve the old relationship and heal our wounds. This mechanism, which is part of the inherent healing capacity of the universe, is also the undoing of many intimate relationships.

The usual response, when our partner reveals him or herself to be just like the old nemesis of our childhood, is to react with the same defenses that we formed in the original relationships. One reason that intimate relationships can produce such intense, protracted fighting is that both partners are so practiced at the particular battle in which they again find themselves. They are each fighting the primal battle of their lives, the stakes being, as they were in childhood, the right both to be loved and to fully exist.

The shift from protective or aggressive reactive behavior to compassion for each other's wounds is a spiritual lesson. It requires us to observe the relationship clearly without becoming lost in the siren's call of our childhood pain. Once we have attuned to the dimension of fundamental consciousness, it becomes much easier to achieve this clarity of perception, and to apply the healing properties of compassion to the problems in our relationship.

So far I have emphasized the importance of having compassion for the psychological wounds of one's partner. For many people, however, it is more difficult to accept compassion than to feel it for someone else. To receive compassion means revealing the fragile, unresolved aspects of ourselves that we usually keep hidden from other people, and sometimes from ourselves as well. Often in a relationship, the give and take of compassion is unbalanced. One partner holds the position of the understanding caretaker, while the other partner maintains the role of needy child. Over time, this imbalance usually results in mutual resentment.

One couple came to work with me because, after several months of living together, they had both found themselves feeling increasingly hostile towards each other. Melissa was a successful novelist with a forceful, direct expressiveness. Sam was a talented painter, but bouts of depression had limited his creative output and the thought of trying to sell his work terrified him. He had an appealing gentleness but seemed preoccupied, as if focused on some indefinable quandary. Melissa's attitude was 'maybe you can help him, I give up'. Sam's attitude was of the noble political prisoner, determined to endure the hour without giving up his secret.

So it was Melissa who told me their story. She said that they had spent a year getting to know each other before moving in together. She had never felt so close to a man before and he had seemed to feel the same towards her. But as soon as Sam had moved into her house, he had begun to brood. She said his depression was like a 'cocoon of dark fog that absorbed him completely'. He complained of her 'overwhelmingly powerful' personality but he depended on her to handle all the details of his life. She paid the bills, made the meals, kept the car running, did the banking, even made dental appointments for him. 'But the worst', Melissa said, beginning to cry, 'is that he won't let me help him feel better. He won't let me comfort him.' At this, Sam seemed to pull even further inward, and it was, as Melissa had described, like fog thickening. 'But you know what?', she said, directing her words towards Sam as if they could pierce through to him, 'I don't buy it. You think you're weaker than I am, but only a very powerful man could create such an impenetrable fortress around himself.'

I agreed with her. Their strength seemed evenly matched, but they needed a way to balance their expression of it. I decided to give them an exercise to do at home that would help them both experience the roles of caretaker and child. The exercise is from a form of psychotherapy called 'reparenting', in which the therapist acts as a stable, loving parent while the client is allowed to regress to early childhood or infancy. This variation for couples works best if there is already a fairly close bond between the partners.

Every day, for several weeks, Melissa and Sam took turns holding and rocking each other. The person being rocked was allowed to become very young and helpless in the other's arms. Sam said that he found it very comforting to surrender to Melissa's maternal embrace. It was also a great relief for him to be allowed to feel deep emotions with another person, without being pressured to verbalize those feelings. Once, during the third week of the exercise, he found himself crying 'just like a baby', trusting the safety of Melissa's love. Melissa said that Sam's trust gave her a sense of extreme tenderness and closeness with him.

It was more difficult for Melissa to be held and rocked by Sam, and for Sam to assume the parental role. In the therapy sessions, Melissa worked with her memories of her parents' 'spaciness', that had caused her to take on the role of caretaker in the family. She remembered waiting for her parents to pick her up after school long after the other parents had come for their children and, in general, feeling abandoned to her own resources. Gradually, she was able to relax her guardedness against this negligence and to let Sam support and nurture her. Sam was very moved to see Melissa so vulnerable. It evoked a new sense of strength and responsibility in him that carried over into his daily life.

The exercise also helped Sam and Melissa communicate more honestly with each other, because they had learned to trust each other's care. When they began to know other details of each other's childhood pain, they felt that they actually knew those children, for they had held and rocked them. They were also able to recognize the wounded child in each other's present behavior. This helped them become more tolerant of each other's difficulties in the relationship.

Intimacy with another person both evokes and alarms the carefully defended, wounded child that has been kept under wraps for so many years. One of the chief requirements of intimate relationships is that we meet this frightened, angry, grieving child with compassion and respect.

COMPASSION FOR GENDER DIFFERENCES

One of the biggest obstacles to intimate relationships between men and women is the difference that exists between male and female thought processes and behavior. In the past few years many writers have described these differences in books such as *He Said, She Said* by Deborah Tannen and *Men are from Mars, Women are from Venus* by John Gray. But no matter how much we read on the subject, it is still astounding to be in relationship with someone we really care about and still come up against a difference in relational style that seems to require the skill of a code-breaker, or to find that our partner has beliefs, values, goals and needs that are very different from our own.

We cannot know for certain to what extent the differences between men and women are innate or culturally conditioned. Surely, many of the differences that were once assumed to be innate now seem to be completely bogus, such as the intellectual and moral inferiority of women suggested by Freud, or the inability of men to nurture their children. It is not difficult to see that millennia of accumulated ignorance and exploitation have resulted in distorted and limited roles for both men and women.

One of the best books to be published on this subject is *I Don't Want to Talk About It* by Terrence Real. He writes,

'Just as girls are pressured to yield that half of their human potential consonant with assertive action, just as they have been systematically discouraged from developing and celebrating the self-concepts and skills that belong to the public world, so are boys pressured to yield attributes of dependency, expressiveness, affiliation – all the self-concepts and skills that belong to the relational, emotive world. These wholesale excisions are equally damaging to the healthy development of both girls and boys. The price for traditional socialization of girls is oppression, as Lyn Brown and Carol Gilligan put it, "the tyranny of the kind and nice". The price of traditional socialization of boys is disconnection – from themselves, from their mothers, from those around them.'[18]

In our society, men are denied their ability to be vulnerable and open to other human beings. Women, by the very pressure that is put on them to be 'nice' and connected with other people, are denied their connection with themselves – they abandon their own needs in order to fulfil the needs of others. Neither the men nor the women in this scenario are capable of intimacy.

The stereotypical division of skills, which robs both men and women of whole facets of their being, also contributes to difficulties in intimacy. When only men are allowed to be competent in their professions, prosperous and assertive, and only women are allowed to be nurturing, intuitive and artistic, the intimacy between them is inevitably hindered by mutual resentment, envy and mistrust. Although we may be attracted to our 'missing half', the natural drive in every human being to be whole will often sabotage a relationship that relies on the sacrifice of our basic potential. I believe that this terrible economy of personal attributes is largely

18 Terrence Real, *I Don't Want To Talk About It* (New York, NY: Fireside, 1997), p.130

responsible for the so called 'battle of the sexes', in which men and women confront the abilities that they have lost with anger, grief and confusion.

Compassion is the solution to the dilemma of gender differences. Just as our lovers carry the wounds of their childhood family, they also carry the frustrations, blindness, expectations, fears and rigid attitudes that result from being a man or a woman in our culture.

To feel compassion for these wounds of gender requires that we shift our perspective to encompass our partner's point of view along with our own. In the last chapter I described the shift in perception from our fragmented self/object stance to perceiving with the all-pervasive space of fundamental consciousness. This spiritual transformation of perception is reflected in our understanding of life as well. Instead of knowing just our own point of view, we begin to see each situation in our lives as a whole, from the vantage point of every person involved.

I had worked for about a year with a man named Jack, who was in his mid-forties and had never had a lasting relationship with a woman. Although he had been very successful in his professional life, and was proud that he had acquired the house, car and bank account that he set out to achieve, he felt that his life was incomplete without a wife. But whenever Jack began a relationship with a woman, he quickly became enraged with her for one reason or another and could no longer tolerate her presence in his life. Since we had begun our work together, I had seen him pass through several of these brief, angry affairs.

One day, hearing him describe the demise of a relationship with yet another infuriating woman, I was struck by the defiant tone of his anger. It was as if he were pitted against a powerful adversary and, in escaping from the relationship, he had gained a hard-won, if bitter, triumph. 'Was she a very powerful woman?', I asked. He answered me with a knowing sneer. 'All women are powerful', he said, as if this were something I already knew. 'All women?', I asked. 'Yes', he said, furiously. 'All women. Women have all the power.' I must have looked incredulous, because he became even more enraged. 'In relationships', he said, as if speaking to a moron, 'Women have all the power in sexual relationships. Women get to decide if it's going to happen or not.'

As he said this, I watched him shape shift – from the powerful businessman that he usually appeared to be, to the intimidated teenaged boy that he once was. Jack had already spent many sessions describing the terrors of his adolescence. He had been a sensitive, intelligent boy; in teenage parlance, a 'nerd'. The boys in his school had attacked him physically and verbally, ridiculing his looks, his name, his clothes, and his claim to heterosexuality. He had not said much about the girls. But now he remembered the utter torment of his early attractions, his clumsy advances and the intense shame and hurt of rejection. He also remembered that he had given up his attempt to approach the girls. He recalled the exact period in his life, in his senior year of high school, when he had retreated into the aloof, scowling, chain-smoking character that had shielded him all these years. As he spoke, his fury weakened, and was replaced by an expression of bewilderment and regret.

We spoke for a while about the rules that are taught us early in life concerning the way men and women, or boys and girls, are supposed to approach each other. We spoke about the pressure on boys to initiate contact, the terrible risk involved in making that first phone call, and then having to provide the girl with a good time, and having to risk rejection again by initiating the first gesture of physical intimacy. And we spoke of how, as the boy gets older, the pressure is on him to please a woman sexually, and of the threat of humiliation if he does not prove himself to be a competent lover. Jack had taken his early fears and failures with women as signs of his personal ineptness. But as we spoke, he began to feel compassion for himself as an adolescent boy, and for men in general, constrained by traditional expectations of manhood that turn the pursuit of love into a daunting obstacle course.

Jack had always resented the power that women have in their traditional role of accepting or declining the man's request for intimacy. I asked Jack if he would like to get some sense of how these cultural roles affect girls and women and when he agreed to this, I asked him to imagine himself as an adolescent girl. Jack struggled with this idea for a moment, but finally he pulled his bulky body into the attitude of a haughty, sensual, teasing girl. Then I asked him to picture an adolescent boy across the room. 'You are very attracted to this boy', I said. 'What are you going to do about it?' Jack intensified his sensual pose, crossing his legs seductively and giving a pretty good imitation of the come-hither expression that most girls learn at an early age. 'Well', I said, 'he has glanced at you and turned away. Now what are you going to do?'

Jack suddenly looked helpless, and slightly ludicrous in his seductive pose, as women often feel when their efforts are ignored. 'Can I call to him?', he asked. 'You can', I answered, 'but that is very forward behavior for a girl. If he rejects you, there will be the added humiliation of having crossed a line, of having transgressed the bounds of feminine decorum, when he was not even interested in you.' 'So I have to wait for him to notice me', said Jack uncrossing his legs and returning, with relief it seemed to me, to his own gender. 'Yes', I said, 'the traditional courting ritual is an "equal opportunity" ordeal.'

Although these traditions are gradually weakening, it will be a while before we are entirely free of their destructive influence. It is therefore important that men and women support each other as we attempt to challenge our mutual history of cultural stereotypes. This means, in particular, that women need to understand the societal pressures on men to be stoic or 'cool', overly responsible and geared for battle. We need to be patient with the incongruities and frustrations that occur as they attempt to become more emotionally vulnerable and responsive. And men need to regard the emergence of female ambition, skill and accomplishment without the reflexive reactions of fear and competitiveness. They need to be patient with the complexities of fragility and strength, need and independence, that women often display as they attempt to become more competent and assertive.

There is a popular notion in our culture, based largely on the writing of Carl Jung, that men have a female aspect and women have a male aspect of personality that needs to be integrated for there to be psychological maturity. These male and female aspects are usually described as personality traits associated with the two genders. I believe this idea has created some confusion. For example, women naturally emit power from the subtle core of their body, just as men do. This quality has been suppressed in women but it still exists as part of their essence. They do not have to get in touch with their 'male side' in order to experience power – they just need to access the core of their own being. And men find that when they soften the defenses in their chest, for example, they are just as emotionally responsive as women. To speak of male and female parts of the personality lends support to the limitations imposed on us by conventional images of gender behavior.

When we inhabit our whole body, we discover that both power and emotion are essential capacities of our being, regardless of our gender. Our anatomy allows us to feel power in our belly and love in our heart at the same time. Thus freedom from the stereotypes of gender helps us to develop the self-contact that is the basis of our contact with each other.

Compassion requires the ability to recognize and appreciate the conflict of authenticity and defense within each person we encounter. This poignant counterpoint of reality and defense is the condition of human life. Although we can grow towards reality, we are never entirely free of this basic human drama. In order to open to the innate movement of compassion, we need to acknowledge and accept this shared condition of humanity.

People who are sensitive to the spiritual aspect of life are usually particularly sensitive and responsive to the world around them. Their ability to see and feel the pain in other people naturally evokes their compassion. However, sensitive people may also suppress their compassion in order to protect themselves from other people's suffering. They may fear that they will be overwhelmed by other people's pain, or that they will have to be responsible for alleviating it, or that the suffering in the world is somehow contagious, that it might diminish the purity and light that they have gained through spiritual practices. Many people have told me that they 'take on' the pain around them, and that this has led to illness.

These fears can prevent people from realizing and living in the dimension of spiritual oneness. However, it is the realization of fundamental consciousness that enables us to be completely open and responsive to life, without mimicking the holding patterns and illnesses of other people. All of the content of life, including the vibrations of emotional and physical pain, literally pass through the clear space of fundamental consciousness without altering it. This means that we can see, feel and respond to other people's pain, but we cannot be injured by it.

When people realize fundamental consciousness, they find that they can finally enjoy the full impact of their sensitivity and compassion for other people. One of the most moving examples that I have witnessed of this transition was a woman named Beth who came to work with me. Beth was a tall, thin woman, who lived and related to the world, from the very top of her superior height. She was extremely courteous towards me, but chillingly distant. Her whole body was pulled in from its periphery, as if to avoid contact with the air around her. Her forehead, however, was brightly lit. From this bright summit, she literally looked down her nose at me.

In the first few months of our work together, we did not get further than the first Subtle Self Work exercise of inhabiting the body. Beth had become accustomed to numbness, and she entered the internal space of her body with extreme caution. She often spent the whole session dwelling in one part of her body, barely breathing, trying to tolerate each new vibration of aliveness. When she was finally able to inhabit her whole body without feeling overwhelmed, we progressed to the exercise of attuning to the qualities of fundamental consciousness – awareness, emotion and sensation – but this exercise was even more difficult for her than the first one. Although she could access the quality of awareness very easily, the instructions to attune to emotion and sensation filled her with terror. She insisted that she would rather discontinue our work than open to these two qualities.

'It just feels like too much', she pleaded with me. 'Too much what?', I asked. 'Too much pain.' 'Your pain?' This question surprised her. Whose pain could it be but her own? I suggested that she attune to the pervasive space of fundamental consciousness, inside and outside her body, and then 'sit' with this question: was it her own pain that seemed to be too much for her?

Beth sat for several minutes, attuned to fundamental consciousness. Then she suddenly pulled herself in, away from the environment, in an extreme version of the holding pattern that she had begun to release over the past few months. 'It's my mother's pain,' she said with effort, 'It's too much for me. I don't want to feel it.' She glanced quickly at the door of my office as if gauging how quickly she could get away, but she remained seated on the couch.

She described to me how her mother had depended on her for emotional support after her father had died, how she had treated Beth as the strong one in the family, someone always available to listen to her troubles. 'But they were too much for me,' she said, looking away from me guiltily. 'I tried at first, but I couldn't help her. As soon as I was old enough, I left home and moved as far away from her as I could.' I pointed out that long before she had been able to escape geographically, she had protected herself from her mother's pain by closing off her emotional responses to the environment.

Beth agreed to 'revisit' her childhood environment in her memory. She attuned again to the pervasive space of fundamental consciousness, and imagined that this space pervaded both herself and the memory of her mother. 'She's a whirlwind of angry, hungry energy', Beth said, beginning to contract again. I suggested that she keep her breath slow and even, and simply observe her mother in the space that pervaded them both. Slowly, Beth relaxed and, concentrating on her breath, was able to sit with the image of her mother. 'She wants me to soothe her,' Beth said, 'but I don't have to. I'm just letting her be there. I'm just letting the whirlwind spin in the space.'

Now I asked Beth to attune to the quality of emotion pervading both herself and her mother. I watched her search for the emotional quality in her chest and then in her whole body. Very carefully, she attuned to the same quality in the space outside of her body, so that the image of her mother was also pervaded by it. After a moment, she began to nod her head, as if she were understanding something for the first time. 'I love her', she said. 'I can't solve her problems but I do love her.' Beth began to cry softly, rocking back and forth as if soothing an infant. An expression of extreme tenderness and compassion came over her face and her body softened. 'I feel sorry for her, and also for myself,' she said, 'I love us both.' The memory of Beth rocking her tall, gaunt body gently on the couch has stayed with me as one of the most beautiful images of compassion that I have ever seen.

EXERCISE 10
LISTENING IN FUNDAMENTAL CONSCIOUSNESS

Partners sit facing each other, either on a chair or cross-legged on a cushion on the floor, with eyes open.

Begin with the exercise for attuning to fundamental conscious-ness: experience that you are inside your whole body all at once. Mentally find the space outside your body, the space in the room. Experience that the space inside and outside of your body is the same, continuous space. Now experience that the space that pervades your body also pervades your partner. Be sure to stay in your own body as you experience this. Keep your breath smooth and even, as you sit together in the unified space of fundamental consciousness.

Take turns with one of you speaking while the other listens. You can time your periods of speaking, so that you each take twenty minutes.

The partner who is listening remains silent and stable in the open space of fundamental consciousness, keeping your breath smooth and even. Experience that the space itself is seeing and hearing your partner.

The speaking partner says whatever occurs to you. If there is something you would like your partner to know or understand about you, you can take this time to express it.

CHAPTER SEVEN

Sexual Intimacy as Spiritual Practice

SEX AND CONTACT

As we realize spiritual oneness, we experience that our own body, and everything around us, is made of unified, fundamental consciousness. This realization is based on a shift in the subtlety and the depth of our internal contact. As consciousness, we are able to experience ourselves all the way through the internal depth of our whole body. In this dimension, as a result of this depth of internal contact, our entire organism is capable of sexual arousal and release.

By attuning to fundamental consciousness during sex, partners can experience contact with themselves and each other at the same time, throughout the whole internal space of their bodies. As I have explained, the mutual contact that two people experience in fundamental consciousness is not just a connection of one body with the other. It is an experience of resonance, of subtle communication, involving awareness, emotion and physical sensation all at the same time. Mutual contact during sex helps deepen both partners' realization of fundamental consciousness, as well as their intimacy with each other, and the intensity of their pleasure.

Just as in other aspects of life, fundamental consciousness does not replace physical matter and energy in the sexual encounter; it includes, pervades and refines them. Sex is still a physical act, of course, involving caressing and the stimulating of erogenous zones, but the caresses become a much more effective means of arousal when they touch through to the actual being of that body, rather than just the physical surface.

Since fundamental consciousness is the most subtle level of ourselves, it is rarely mentioned in the psychological or even the spiritual literature on sexuality. Although most people agree that they enjoy sex more when there is tenderness or love between partners, the sex act itself is generally viewed as purely physical. Sexual pleasure is regarded as the result of physical friction between the partners' sexual organs without mention of actual contact between the sexual organs. Even traditional spiritual sex practices often emphasize the physical level, focusing on strange postures that can be assumed, or the number and phrasing of 'strokes' of the penis within the vagina to which men are advised to aspire. This is based on the understanding that the chief requirement for sexual 'success' is that the man maintain his erection for long periods of time. Naturally, many men accomplish this task by diverting their attention elsewhere during sex, but when the man is distracted, both the pleasure and the spiritual potential of the sexual encounter is reduced.

The Indian, Tibetan and Chinese spiritual traditions also contain more subtle sexual exercises which emphasize the energy dimension. These teach the exchange of energy between partners during sex, as well as ways to send the energy of sexual arousal up through the subtle core of the body towards the brain.[19] When sexual sensation reaches the brain, it produces an experience of ecstatic release. Although these exercises work with energy, they can deepen and expand our realization of fundamental consciousness because they help

19 The traditional and Subtle Self Work sex exercises are effective for both heterosexual and same-sex partners. Any two people who experience the excitement of sexual arousal can apply that excitement to spiritual realization.

open the subtle core of the body, our entranceway into spiritual oneness. The Tibetan Buddhist teacher, Lama Thubten Yeshe, wrote, 'Practice with a consort causes the airs to enter the central channel more strongly; and the more strongly the airs enter, the more strongly they will stabilize and absorb, and the more bliss will be generated. The purpose of practicing with a consort is to increase these experiences, and eventually to energize complete absorption of the winds at the heart chakra, total bliss, and total realization of nonduality.'[20]

The importance of the energy dimension for sexual intimacy has also been recognized by many schools of psychotherapy. In the fifties, Wilhem Reich developed a method of psychotherapy that emphasized sexual energy, believing that psychological health was measured by how fully someone could experience orgasm. A truly healthy person would experience the release and pleasure of orgasm throughout his or her whole body. Reich's method, called orgone therapy, focused on freeing the energy system by releasing the psychological defenses that bind and diminish it.

Just as in other aspects of relationship, however, if partners remain in the energy dimension, they do not reach the deepest level of either intimacy or spiritual realization. The energy dimension, although of great importance to sexual intimacy, is just a partial aspect of sexual experience. Even during sexual union, the oneness that we experience in fundamental consciousness is very different than the merging that occurs in the energy dimension. Instead of the 'zoned out' feeling of merging, there is an experience of presence and clarity throughout the bodies of both partners.

Also, as fundamental consciousness, we can remain present as the spontaneous flow of arousal moves through our own

20 Lama Thubten Yeshe, *The Bliss of Inner Fire* (Somerville, MA: Wisdom Publications, 1998), p.166

body and the body of our partner, building towards orgasm. This helps increase our threshold for sexual sensation, because if we swoon into semi-consciousness at the first whiff of pleasure, we limit our potential for arousal and release. In this dimension, we are able to remain present even during the release of orgasm. This does not mean that we watch the experience of release, as if we were somehow separate from it; but that our consciousness pervades the movement and ecstasy of release. This enables us to experience the full impact of sexual pleasure. It also enables us to integrate the movement of energetic release with the stillness of fundamental conscious-ness. This helps us integrate fundamental consciousness with the movement of all of our life experience.

Many sexual difficulties can be resolved when we experience internal contact with ourselves and our partner in fundamental consciousness. For example, both men and women can experience a greater intensity of sexual pleasure if they inhabit and contact each other through the internal space of their genitals. Mutual genital contact also helps couples match each other's intensity of pleasure, so that the duration of the sexual encounter is satisfying for both partners.

Many sensitive people guard against sexual arousal because they are afraid of being overwhelmed by sensation. A couple once came to work with me because, in the five years that they had been together, they had never been able to enjoy having sex together. It was the wife, Paula, who had persuaded her husband, Anthony to come to therapy. She complained that Anthony never initiated sex with her, and when she initiated it, he almost always rebuffed her. He did not even like her to touch him affectionately. Anthony agreed that he did not like to be touched 'all of a sudden', and wanted her to 'warn' him before she approached.

When they did have sex, Anthony reached orgasm almost

immediately, and this too felt like a rejection to Paula, as if he wanted to get it over with as quickly as possible. Paula said that Anthony's rejection of her made her feel unattractive, and she constantly demanded that he admit to his attraction to other women. But Anthony insisted that he did find Paula attractive; it was just difficult for him to be close to someone physically. Paula had also persuaded Anthony to see several hypnotists and psychics, to find out if he had ever been sexually abused, but there did not seem to be any history of sexual violation in Anthony's past.

Paula was a sprightly, quick-witted woman in her thirties, capable of humorous repartee even while she was crying. Anthony, about ten years older, had a remarkably gentle, lyrical voice and a penetrating gaze that was usually directed towards the floor, or the window behind me. As they spoke about their relationship, Paula sprawled on the couch, an arm or a leg extended towards Anthony, while Anthony sat almost primly upright, his hands placed carefully on his knees. It seemed to me that there was something deliberate about Anthony's self-containment, as if it were a practiced skill. I noticed that he tightened his posture, ever so slightly, every time Paula shifted her position on the couch, and I had the sense that he was extremely aware of her physicality.

One session, about a month after we had first met, I asked them to sit across the room from each other, as far apart as they could get from each other in my office. Then I asked Paula to stroke Anthony's body from where she sat. Although she was a little puzzled by this instruction, she faced Anthony and began to caress the air. To her surprise, she was able to feel that she was actually touching him. And Anthony was also able to feel her touch. For the first time, I saw Anthony relax his guard and receive the sensation of Paula's caress. When they reversed roles, Anthony could easily touch Paula from across the room, and Paula found that if she attuned very subtly to the space between them, she could also feel Anthony's touch. They enjoyed this exercise very much, and Paula joked that they had finally found a way to have sex, but when they did attempt to have sex that night, Anthony again recoiled from Paula's touch.

In the following sessions, I taught them how to inhabit their bodies and experience oneness with each other in fundamental consciousness at the same time. We also continued the exercise of them caressing each other across space. As they became adept at inhabiting their own bodies, Anthony was able to receive the stimulation of Paula's touch at closer range. Finally he was able to allow her to put her hand on his body itself. They practiced touching each other, and receiving each other's touch, beginning with less sexually responsive parts of the body, such as the arm or lower leg. One would rest their hand on the other's body, while the other person practiced inhabiting that area and opening to the sensation of the touch.

During this process, Anthony remembered the all-encompassing, possessive nature of his mother's embrace. He was able to observe how he 'closed up' his skin when he thought of her touch. Although no one would equate the embraces of a loving mother with sexual abuse, Anthony, as a very sensitive child, had been over-stimulated, and his budding connection to himself overwhelmed, by his mother's affection.

After several months had passed, I gave Paula and Anthony a new exercise to practice at home. I asked them to lie next to each other, side by side, and to practice inhabiting their whole body, and receiving each other's touch throughout their whole body. They then progressed to practicing the same exercise facing each other. I emphasized that they should wait for sexual arousal to occur spontaneously, and not to have sex unless that happened. This constraint was difficult for Paula, but it helped relieve Anthony's anxiety about having to perform sexually. Finally, they both were able to relax and receive the stimulation of each other's touch, and sexual arousal did occur. They also found that Anthony was able to sustain his arousal longer when he inhabited his genital area. This allowed him to tolerate and to build a much greater intensity of pleasure than he had ever experienced before. One morning I received an e-mail from Anthony which read 'This must be what all the fuss is about.'

The exploration of sexual healing and freedom was, I believe, one of the most important enterprises of the twentieth century. Since my adolescence in the sixties, I have been familiar with the various rigors of this quest; I know what courage and personal strength is needed to challenge one's own inhibitions and fears. I have also seen the self-destructive edge of this pursuit, the overuse of sensation-enhancing drugs, the despair over one's sexual deficiencies, and the bitterness of a hunger stimulated but never quite satisfied. I think that the missing element in much of this sexual exploration has been a knowledge of our spiritual essence as the basis of contact and sexual pleasure.

A man once came to work with me who had devoted the previous three decades of his life to the pursuit of 'great sex'. In his fifties, Bill had long, wildly curling gray hair, and he always wore sensual fabrics like silk in bright colors, and silver jewelry. I recognized him at once, as one old hippy to another. Beneath the colorful bandana wrapped around his head, however, his eyes held an unchanging grimness that reflected his long, disappointing odyssey.

Bill felt that if he could experience a truly satisfying sexual encounter, it would empower him in every aspect of his life.

To this end he had attended countless workshops, learned an array of sexual techniques, and engaged in many different types of sexual orgy. With the help of drugs and alcohol, his sexual adventures had become increasingly wild, but even though he was finally able to feel fairly at ease writhing naked among a group of people, he did not experience much actual pleasure in these encounters. Furthermore, when he attempted to have sex with someone one-on-one, his old inhibitions seemed to come right back.

Although Bill was willing to practice the Subtle Self Work exercises, and was able to experience the pervasive space of fundamental consciousness fairly quickly, he dismissed my suggestions about the nature of intimacy. After several months, he announced that he was going to Thailand, something he 'should have done years ago', to find the prostitute who would finally liberate him from his sexual conundrum. He returned two weeks later, with a puzzled and somewhat tender expression in his eyes, and a little more interested in learning about contact. He told me that when he arrived at the establishment in Thailand they showed him a line-up of women from which to choose. Without hesitation, he pointed to the youngest one, a delicate beauty, new to the job. He had always resented the legal and moral restraints in America that had kept him from the benefits of sex with someone so young. He was sure that this very young woman would have sufficient vitality to satisfy him. But when they were alone, he suddenly noticed the terror in her eyes. Although she allowed him to enter her, he could feel the fear in her body and he said that he had never been so aware of the other person in bed with him. Although she was not able to give him the sexual ecstasy that he craved, she did help him begin to heal his sexuality. Her fear and vulnerability compelled him to abandon his anxieties about himself and his demand to be satisfied, and attune to the presence of another human being.

SEXUALITY AND WHOLENESS

The development of our sexuality is necessary for spiritual realization because it is part of the wholeness of our organism. I do not mean that we must be sexually active in order to realize fundamental consciousness, but we do need to release the defenses that repress our sexuality in order to reach the subtle core of our whole body. We cannot realize the wholeness and unity of fundamental consciousness if we do not include our sexuality, and our essential quality of physical sensation, in our subtle attunement to ourselves. As I have said, for many people the physical sensation aspect of fundamental consciousness is the most difficult to access. Sexual repression is passed down from one generation to the next through education and example. This legacy has left us, as a society, relatively numb to the pleasure of touch and sexual arousal.

Since the latter half of the twentieth century, however, we have begun to heal and regain this lost part of ourselves. The fortunate encounter of Western psychological understanding with Eastern spiritual teachings has taught us the value of nature, and the basic unity and interdependence of the various parts of nature. In our time, even the medical profession has begun to accept the relationship between our physical functions, our emotions and our thoughts. Sexuality, once thought to be the base hunger of the body alone, is seen in this new light as belonging to, and affecting, our whole nature.

This must necessarily transform our spiritual understanding as well. If there is no true separation between our physical nature and our spiritual nature, then our sexuality is part of our spiritual nature. To attempt to transcend our sexuality produces a fragmentation in us, a schism that is experienced as tension and incompleteness, often leading to illness and depression. The experience of wholeness that occurs when we accept our sexuality as belonging to our essential, spiritual nature is one of the hallmarks of the new spiritual understanding that is presently emerging.

Both Western psychology and Eastern religion have helped generate the perception of spiritual realization as a process of becoming whole. The Eastern religions contribute to this understanding because they teach us that our true nature is spiritual. Eastern spiritual methods seek to uncover our reality from the distortions that mask it, just as modern Western psychology seeks to uncover our true humanity from the repression that binds it.

Western psychology has been engaged, since it began with Sigmund Freud, with the subject of sexuality. Freud was fascinated by the co-existence of our instinctive nature with the transcendent artifice of civilization. He felt that people became psychologically ill when their unruly instincts threatened to break out of their civilizing containment, and he saw his job as helping people to sublimate them. Only gradually has the emphasis in the field of psychology shifted from the bolstering of all that is civilized in us, to the salvage of all that is natural. Wilhem Reich, with his intuitive understanding of the completely orgasmic person, was one of the first Western psychologists to recognize the importance of sexual health for personal maturity. A completely enlightened person would be completely orgasmic, as Reich surmised. I am not sure that Reich knew how rare it is that someone achieves the total freedom that he envisioned, but I believe he was correct about the direction of the journey.

The relatively inclusive attitude of Eastern religion towards sexuality has also helped loosen our society's association of sexual 'purity' with the spiritual life. The Trappist monk, Thomas Merton, tells a funny story in his *Asian Journal*. One of the people he visited in India, in 1968, was the director of the International Academy of Indian Culture. At the end of his visit, he was given the choice of several cloths printed with *mandalas*, symbolic images used for meditation. Merton chose one that he said attracted him as being 'very lively'. When he examined it more closely, he found that it was covered with tiny images of men and women having sexual intercourse. He writes, 'On close inspection I find it to be full of copulation, which is all right but I don't quite know how one meditates on it. It might be a paradoxical way to greater purity.'[21] This design of 'copulation' is known in Buddhism as 'deities in union'. The woman faces the man with her legs wound around his hips and her head thrown back as if in extreme sexual excitement. It is one of the most sacred images of Tibetan Buddhism and is used in their advanced visualization practices.

Recently, I attended a ceremony at a Tibetan Buddhist monastery near my home in Woodstock, NY. The monastery belongs to the Kagyu lineage of Buddhism, which has been compared to the Catholic Church in its use of elaborate ritual and ornate decor. The ceremony was called an 'empowerment' because it authorizes and prepares the participants to do a particular practice, this one being dedicated to the Medicine Buddha. The practice involves a combination of devotional prayers and transformative techniques.

The officiating lama was Khenpo Karthar Rinpoche, the Abbot of the monastery, an old man of great dignity. He sat at

---

21 Thomas Merton, *The Asian Journal of Thomas Merton* (New York: New Directions Books, 1968), p.66

the front of the shrine room on an elevated chair decorated with rich brocades, while the sixty or so participants sat cross-legged on cushions, facing him. In the main event of the ceremony, the lama gave us the blessing of the Medicine Buddha for our 'body, speech and mind'. For this, he came down from his throne and walked slowly and majestically among us with an object containing a picture of the Medicine Buddha. First, however, he told us that he would touch our head and our hands with this object, and then we were, with our own hands, to touch our throat, heart, navel and genitals. So each of us, having been blessed by this venerable man in robes, solemnly touched our body, including our genitals, as he passed by. As I put my hands on my own genitals, I thought how odd this would seem in a Catholic Church.

But, for the Tibetan Buddhists, it was gravely important that one's whole being receive the empowering influence of the blessing.

SEX AND REALITY

Fundamental consciousness is our true nature, the dimension of authenticity. When we bring this dimension into our sexual intimacy we experience authentic connection with each other. As in all aspects of life, everyone wants to be authentic in sex but it is not so easy. From our earliest years, our family, friends and culture teach us very specific ideas about what sex should be like, and what men and women should be like during sex. The whole event, from seduction to the sex act itself is often, as erotic writer Marco Vassi described it, a 'little bit of theater'[22]. We are prepared for our roles in this production long before we can make an

---

22 Marco Vassi, *Woodstock Times*, circa 1981

informed choice in the matter. By the time we are adults, the characters that we play, and the attitudes that we project towards potential lovers, can easily be mistaken for our true nature, because they have become chronic holding patterns in our body.

As children and adolescents, we distort our bodies to conform to the 'attitude' of femaleness or maleness that we see in our parents, teachers and media stars. Boys may mimic the aloof, stoic quality of the men they admire by literally locking themselves up within their bodies, constricting their emotional responses until they truly become as cool and alienated as most of our male cultural heroes. Or they may chronically inflate their chests or thrust forward with their heads in an imitation of aggressive male authority. During sex, this male stereotype is compelled to maintain both dominance and self-control. In relationship with a woman who has been taught to passively receive the sexual event, his role becomes a high stakes solo.

A woman may chronically constrict her intellect in order to make herself more 'approachable', and tighten her throat to stop expressions of opinion or anger. She may try to conform to the standard image of feminine sexual allure by chronically holding in her stomach muscles, lifting her chest and exaggerating the protrusion of her behind. In the movie *Female Perversions*, based on the book by psychologist Louise A. Kaplan, a woman explains to a young girl that she did not know how to be feminine when she was young. As the girl watches in fascination and horror, the woman gyrates her hips in a graceless, exaggerated dance of seduction. 'It takes a while to get it, but you will', the woman promises, with just a hint of threat in her voice. Almost all girls grow up objectifying their bodies; presenting a prepared image of themselves to the appraising gaze of the world, while they hide out elsewhere. They become the object rather than the subject. In order to be a successful object during sex, a woman must continue to project a sexy image, which may entirely distract her from experiencing her actual sexual sensation.

As we grow up learning the artifices of the men and women around us, we also become imprinted with the troubled ways in which these two genders relate with each other. One of the most common patterns of misinteraction can be described as the relationship between a sponge and a stone. The woman, who is open and responsive emotionally but feeling no sense of her own existence, looks desperately to her male partner for the emotional response she believes she needs in order to feel alive. The man, who is already conditioned to suppress his emotions, feels that his own life substance is threatened by the absorbing neediness of the woman, and barricades himself against her demands with all of his will. This 'catch-22' of male-female relationship has dire consequences in the arena of sexual intimacy. There can be no contact or energetic flow, no exchange of pleasure, between a stone and a sponge.

Another type of confusion generated by the encounter of male and female images was illustrated by a married couple who came to work with me. In the first session they volleyed a multitude of complaints against each other, which could be reduced to two main and somewhat contradictory themes. Sylvia was upset with her husband's fondness for pornographic magazines and his ogling of attractive women whenever they went out together. 'He's attracted to body parts', she told me with a sneer. Simon's main complaint was his wife's obsession with her appearance. 'She has to put on make-up to mail a letter half a block from our house.' 'She has to try three outfits on before we can go out, and I'm supposed to tell her how great she looks in them. If I make any criticism at all, we never get out the door.'

Sylvia was particularly hurt by Simon's looking at other women. Her response was complex, she said. She felt that she could not measure up to the women that Simon admired, and she also felt 'chilled' that his attention could be claimed by something as 'impersonal' as a well-shaped body. Simon felt that Sylvia was overreacting. He said that all men looked at women, that it was perfectly natural and had no bearing on his feelings for Sylvia.

This conflict between them also affected their sexual intimacy. Sylvia said that Simon was 'in some sort of daze' when they made love. 'He looks away; it's as if he's not even really touching me.' Simon asked what she meant by this and Sylvia explained, 'I can tell that you don't really feel me when you touch me.' Simon complained that Sylvia was also in 'some other state' during sex. 'It's like she's putting on an act. She makes all kinds of sounds, but it's not really sexy because it doesn't seem real.' This made Sylvia furious. Who was he, she asked, to talk about reality. She was just trying to make herself seem sexier because she knew she was competing with some fantasy in his head about the ideal woman. She accused him of fantasizing about other women when they made love. 'Admit it', she demanded. At this Simon looked embarrassed, and conceded that he usually did picture a woman that he had seen in a magazine or on the street. 'It just makes it more exciting,' he said. 'Not for me', Sylvia countered.

They kept returning to this theme in the following sessions, and it became clear that this was the major source of discord in their relationship. Simon continued to ridicule Sylvia's concern about her appearance, and Sylvia continued to complain about Simon's attentions to other women. Then one day they came to their session in a particular state of fury. They had gotten to my town a little early and had gone to a coffee shop nearby. The young waitress serving them had

worn a miniskirt and Simon had apparently followed her
with his eyes as she went about her work during the whole
twenty minutes or so that they were there. 'He doesn't just
look,' Sylvia told me. 'It's as if he's fixated. Otherwise he
would know he was hurting my feelings and stop. I mean, he
can look all he wants when we're not together. But once he's
focused on some woman, it's as if I'm not even there. He
can't control it. And it doesn't even matter how pretty the
woman is. He responds to the act.'

She looked at me to see if I knew what she meant by 'the
act'. I did. Instead of the angry rejoinder that I expected from
Simon, he looked thoughtful. 'I guess that's true,' he said. 'It
is like a fixation. That's why I don't like when you dress up
like that.' 'Why?', asked Sylvia. 'Because I feel manipulated.
Like I have to respond in a certain way.'

This is another unhappy paradox of conventional male-
female relationships. Men often feel manipulated by the
constant barrage of erotic female images served up in the
media and imitated by girls and women. Yet women try to
become these images because men respond to them. The
extreme sexual objectification of women gives rise to the
image of woman as both slave and manipulator of men, and
to the image of man as both dominator and victim of women.
Although it most likely is natural for heterosexual men to
look at women, and for women to enjoy the attention of men,
the cultural exaggeration of this motif creates an artificial
posturing on both sides that obscures our actual attraction to
each other.

Simon described feeling pleasantly 'fed' by the women he
stared at in magazines or on the street, but he was also aware
of anger towards them, anger at feeling pushed towards
sexual arousal by their eroticized mannerisms, and at the
expectation of response that was the measure of his manhood.

He also resented having to reassure Sylvia about her appearance, and he felt confused and guilty about his awareness of her physical flaws. Sylvia, for her part, felt insecure about her ability to compete with the attractiveness of the women Simon looked at, even when she recognized their sexuality as contrived and superficial. She knew that she would never have the perfect body that Simon seemed to be looking for, and she feared that as she aged, she would lose his attention altogether.

As Simon and Sylvia began to discuss these issues with each other, they realized that they were both trapped in the same cultural myth. In order to heal their relationship, they needed to see through these images of male and female seduction to the actual sexuality of their own bodies. Simon found that by allowing himself to look clearly at the women around him, he could free himself of the manipulation of their sexy 'act'. Sylvia discovered that by inhabiting her own body, particularly her sexual anatomy, she had an ongoing felt sense of her true attractiveness.

Many people fear that if they let go of their embodied gender image, they will no longer be attractive to the opposite sex. Stereotypical behaviors, such as an attitude of dim-wittedness or helplessness in women, or an attitude of authority or invulnerability in men, are like codes that we have learned in order to convey sexual appeal. For actual contact to occur between people, it is necessary to trade these codes for the specificity of real communication, to go beyond the beaming of images to the actual encounter of two human beings. The courage to make this shift emerges out of spiritual love, by which I mean the love of reality. When we inhabit our gender as a quality of being, rather than as theater, we may not draw the attention of every man or woman we meet, but we will attract those people who truly excite us.

EXERCISE 11
DEVELOPING CONTACT DURING SEX

Partners touch each other's hands palm to palm.

Maintaining this touch, feel that you inhabit your own hand. Feel how this changes the quality of contact between you. Let yourselves experience the contact between your hands.

Experience that you inhabit your lips. Feel the contact of your upper lip against your lower lip.

Still inhabiting your own lips, touch your lips to your partner's lips. Experience the contact between your lips. Slowly move your lips along your partner's lips, maintaining contact.

Partners can practice this exercise with any parts of the body. Experience that you inhabit your genitals. Touch your genitals to your partner's genitals. Heterosexual couples should practice this with the man's penis inside of the woman's vagina. Experience the contact between your genitals. Practice maintaining this contact while moving your genitals against your partner's genitals.

Either standing up or lying down, feel that you inhabit your whole body all at once.

Staying inside your own body, touch the whole front of your body to your partner's body. Experience the contact between your bodies. Staying within your own body, experience that you contact the whole internal space of your partner's body.

EXERCISE 12
THE 'SECRET' CHAKRA

Tibetan Buddhism mentions an important chakra, called the 'secret' chakra, for intensifying sexual pleasure. It is located at the tip of the penis and at the top of the vagina. You can develop this chakra by penetrating into it with your focus, and breathing into it. Let your breath be very subtle (it feels like a mixture of breath and mind) as you do this.

EXERCISE 13
STRENGTHENING THE PC MUSCLE

This exercise strengthens the pubococcygeal muscle at the base of the torso. Most experts on sexuality agree that the strength of this muscle is crucial for sexual pleasure in both men and women. You can locate this muscle by imagining that you are stopping the flow of urine. Then contract and release this area, beginning with just a few repetitions at a time and progressing to as many as feels comfortable. This exercise becomes more powerful if you inhale on the contraction, hold your breath and the contraction as long as you can comfortably, and then release your breath and the muscle at the same time.

EXERCISE 14
CORE ATTUNEMENT DURING SEX

This is the main spiritual sex exercise of Subtle Self Work. It can help both to free the upward energy through the subtle core of the body, and to bring both partners into the dimension of spiritual oneness.

Lie facing each other with either partner on top or with both of

you on your sides. Heterosexual partners should do the exercise
with the man's penis inside the woman's vagina.

Both partners follow these instructions at the same time.

Experience that you are inside your whole body all at once. Find
the space outside your body. Experience that the space pervading
your body also pervades the body of your partner. Be sure to
remain inside your own body as you do this.

Maintain your attunement to fundamental consciousness
pervading both your bodies as you begin stimulating each other
through genital contact and movement.

When you are both aroused, stop moving and find your first
chakra, at the base of your spine. Bring your focus deeply and
precisely within the subtle core of the first chakra. From your
own first chakra, find your partner's first chakra. Stay in your
own first chakra as you do this.

Find the chakra at the tip of the penis, or the top of the vagina.
Bring your focus precisely into this point. From this chakra, find
the corresponding chakra of your partner.

Find your second chakra, in the innermost core of your sacral
area. From your own second chakra, find your partner's second
chakra. Experience the energy of your sexual arousal move up
through your core to your second chakra. Do not pull the energy
upward; the energy will rise upward by itself if you open to it. If
this does not happen right away, it will with practice.

Find your third chakra, on the level of your navel but in the
subtle core of your body. From your own third chakra, find your

partner's third chakra. Experience the energy of your sexual arousal move up through your core to your third chakra.

If you lose your sensation of sexual arousal, begin again to stimulate each other through genital contact and movement. When you feel sufficiently aroused, you can continue the attunement exercise.

Find your heart chakra, in the innermost subtle core of your chest. From your own heart chakra, find your partner's heart chakra. Experience the energy of your sexual arousal move up through your core to your heart chakra.

Find your throat chakra, in the innermost subtle core of your throat. From your own throat chakra, find your partner's throat chakra. Experience the energy of your sexual arousal move up through your core to your throat chakra.

Find the center of your head. From the center of your head, find the center of your partner's head. Experience the energy of your sexual arousal move up through your core to the center of your head.

Find your seventh chakra, at the center of the top of your head. From your own seventh chakra, find your partner's seventh chakra. Experience the energy of your sexual arousal move up through your whole core to your seventh chakra.

Epilogue

There is an Indian story of a king who was looking for a spiritual teacher. Many renowned sages and scholars applied for the position, but the king rejected them. Finally one man, humble in appearance and seemingly out of place in the rich court, approached the throne. Instead of expounding his spiritual knowledge, the man looked deeply into the king's eyes. The king knelt before this man and began to weep. He had found his teacher.

Human beings know instinctively that the ability to love is more valuable than any other accomplishment. The path of personal and spiritual growth leads towards the ability for genuine contact. This is a transformation of our entire organism. The body softens and becomes available for pleasure, the heart opens and becomes available for feeling and the mind clears and becomes available for understanding. We no longer meet the world at the surface of ourselves, but through the subtle, internal depth of our whole being. As we learn the spiritual lessons of compassion and non-grasping, as we trace our way backward through the labyrinth of our psychological defenses, as we attune inward to the subtlest realm of our being, we are transformed into lovers of life.